CW01496762

LEAKY GUT NO MORE

18 Proven Ways to Heal Leaky Gut Naturally

Boost Metabolism and Lose Weight Permanently.

Look And Feel Great!

by Sarah Jones

New Revised and Improved 2020 Edition

New Recipes Included

Leaky Gut No More Copyright © 2020 by

Salt&PepperPublishing

www.Salt&PepperPublishing.com

DISCLAIMER

N o part of this publication may be reproduced or transmitted in any form or by any means, mechanical or electronic, including photocopying or recording, or by any information storage and retrieval system, or transmitted by email without permission in writing from the publisher.

While all attempts have been made to verify the information provided in this publication, neither the author nor the publisher assumes any responsibility for errors, omissions, or contrary interpretations of the subject matter herein.

This book is for entertainment purposes only. The views expressed are those of the author alone and should not be taken as expert instruction or commands. The reader is responsible for his or her actions.

Adherence to all applicable laws and regulations, including international, federal, state, and local governing professional licensing, business practices, advertising, and all other aspects of doing business in the US, Canada, or any other jurisdiction is the sole responsibility of the purchaser or reader.

Neither the author nor the publisher assumes any responsibility or liability whatsoever on the behalf of the purchaser or reader of these materials. Any perceived slight of any individual or

TABLE OF CONTENT

INTRODUCTION

T he book you are holding, *Leaky Gut No More,* has one goal; to help you heal your gut in a simple, natural and sustainable way that is easy to achieve in everyday life.

If you are tired of brain fog, constant fatigue, low energy, bloated and swollen belly no matter what you eat, mood swings, depression, overeating and inability to lose weight, then this book will show you dietary and lifestyle changes to start feeling better fast.

The book is 100% action-oriented and written in plain English (not overwhelming and not too scientific).

The number one reason why people fail to fix their digestive problems is because they are overwhelmed by advice, which leads to paralysis by analysis. So, instead of telling you to do 20 things the very first day, we only recommend the very best and proven to work ideas.

We are going to focus entirely on what you can do now and in the nearest future to fix your gut and give your intestinal health a good kick to bring back your optimal health.

With a *Leaky Gut No More*, you receive a handbook explaining the causes, triggers and symptoms of a leaky gut that will help you to better understand how to fix it and prevent it from recurring.

You also benefit from a detailed list of foods you should and shouldn't eat, together with extra tips to speed up your healing process.

You are getting a simple and strategic action plan followed by proven to work healing recipes, supplements, and ideas supporting your healing mindset. And many more. All to make the process as easy and doable as possible.

We have provided only the tips and ideas that are effective, skipping hundreds of tips that we haven't tested. All the ideas are to help you heal your intestinal health without ruining your budget.

Your gut will thank you for getting a copy of this book. Aside from healing leaky gut and boosting your immune system, you are going to learn how to build a truly gut-healing lifestyle based on building better habits and daily routines supporting the process.

The recipes included here are not only delicious and gut-healing but also made with real foods, containing plenty of nutrients your body needs to heal your gut, such as vitamins A, D, E, C, fatty acids, enzymes, zinc, sulfur, selenium, L-Glutamine, collagen, and anti-oxidants. They are designed to help you rebuild the microbiome, lose unwanted fat, improve your cognitive health, lift spirits and get more sustainable energy. The recipes are packed with everyday ingredients to save on cost, simple – that means they work for any cooking ability, and made with love.

Let this book become your companion in your personal journey towards long-lasting and sustainable wellness.

CHAPTER 1

WHAT IS LEAKY GUT SYNDROME AND HOW IT IMPACTS YOUR HEALTH

B efore we get down to the nitty gritty, we should first understand what leaky gut is and how it affects our overall health. All in plain words, of course.

So, what is a Leaky Gut Syndrome?

Leaky Gut Syndrome (aka: Intestinal Permeability) is a condition in which gaps in your intestinal wall start to loosen.

As a result, larger substances, such as toxins, undigested food, bacteria, viruses and parasites easily pass across the intestinal wall into the bloodstream.

The immune system considers those substances as pathogens and attacks them.

This leads to an immune response that may manifest in any of the signs of leaky gut discussed below.

Millions of people suffer from leaky gut syndrome not even knowing about it.

While it may seem that leaky gut affects "only" the digestive system, research states that it actually often leads to non-digestion-related health problems such as chronic fatigue syndrome, Alzheimer's, arthritis, multiple sclerosis, depression, and many more. Leaky gut is one of the most common contributors in nearly every inflammation condition.

The cause of low energy, food allergies, joint pain, autoimmune conditions, slow metabolism, and thyroid disease could also be the progression of leaky gut symptoms.

The gut is inherently permeable to small molecules in order to absorb their nutrients. Regulating intestinal permeability, in fact, is the cells' basic function, and occurs in the intestinal wall.

Gluten in sensitive people can cause the cells in the gut to release the protein Zonulin, which can break apart the intestinal lining's tight junctions. Other factors such as toxins, infection, age, and stress, also cause the junctions to split apart. Once the junctions break, your gut starts "leaking".

Leaky Gut Causes

The main culprits of Leaky Gut Syndrome include:

- Infections

- Toxins *

- Inflammatory foods causing your gut to become leaky: grains – particularly wheat/gluten, legumes, refined sugar, commercial dairy, processed food, starches, unhealthy vegetable oils, margarines.

- Age

- Chronic stress (this one is crucial and causes serious damage in the gut)

- Candida overgrowth

- Parasites

*Toxins usually come in the form of:

- Antibiotics,

- Steroids,

- Acid-reducing drugs,

- NSAIDs like Advil and Motrin

- They are also present in BPA from plastics, mercury, and environmental toxins like mercury.

A Closer Look at How Our Body Digests Food

Digestion starts in the mouth, which secretes saliva through the salivary glands. Saliva is made of filtered blood, with the red blood cells eliminated. Moreover, calcium, hormones, and parts of the immune system in the saliva help you chew.

Proper chewing breaks up food chunks, making it easy to digest. The tongue provides the brain sensory information and tells you whether the food you ate is good or bad. The tongue is also an essential part of the immune system.

The lingual tonsils (the bumps at the tongue's root) analyze whatever passes through them. Immune cells investigate whether the substance that passes through is beneficial or hazardous and alerts the immune system if the substance poses a hazard.

Upon swallowing, food goes down the esophagus, which is a muscular tube that contracts and expands in a wave-like manner. Such actions facilitate easy movement of food into the stomach. The esophagus hooks a right turn into the stomach, ending in the lower esophageal sphincter. This is a link between the esophagus and the stomach. The sphincter stops stomach juices and food from going back up.

The stomach is located under the lungs and heart. The stomach has defenses from the juices, enzymes, and acids found within it to help in breaking down food. The esophagus, however, does not have the same defensive action. When juices and food end up in the esophagus (also called reflux), it leads to a burning sensation or pressure and pain in your chest.

The stomach breaks down the food before the food goes through the small intestine, which stretches from three to six meters. The small intestine continues digestion and breaks down the food into smaller particles. The pancreas and liver secrete juices that help in food breakdown.

Microscopic villi line the small intestine. In turn, more microvilli line the first layer of villi. They catch the partially digested food that comes their way. The microvilli also help increase the digestive tract's surface area, and maximizing the change to absorb and digest important nutrients.

The microvilli absorb the digested molecules, which pass through the bloodstream before heading for the liver. The liver screens the digested molecules and nutrients before they can pass through the circulatory system. Whatever substance remains that does not enter the liver enters the colon or large intestine, which main purpose is to break down the remaining particles and eliminate water from waste, which is ready for excretion.

The large intestine's surface is different from that of the small intestine. The colon depends on bacteria to break down the remaining particles. Thus, the large intestine is where most of the gut bacteria reside. The small intestine has roughly 100,000 bacteria for every ¼ teaspoon of content. On the other hand, the large intestine has 20 billion bacteria for every ¼ teaspoon of content.

Moreover, **it takes 16 hours for the large intestine to process a meal**, which leaves the small intestine the job of processing the succeeding meals. The liver first filters any absorbed nutrients before they enter the circulatory system. The small intestine is also the location where you absorb vital minerals like calcium and vitamins like riboflavin, B12, and K.

At the end of the digestive journey, what passes through the large intestine goes to the rectum and passes out the meal as feces. With that basic biological recap of how digestion works, it is time to know what could go wrong in the digestive process.

What are the Symptoms of a Leaky Gut

So, how do you know if you are experiencing a leaky gut syndrome?

Symptoms you need to look out for include:

- Asthma

- Seasonal allergies

- Bloating

- Gas

- IBS (Irritable Bowel Syndrome)

- Diarrhea

- Hormonal imbalances like PCOS (polycystic ovarian syndrome) or PMS (premenstrual syndrome)

- Autoimmune disorders: Hashimoto's thyroiditis, rheumatoid arthritis, psoriasis, celiac disease, or lupus

- Fibromyalgia

- Chronic fatigue

- Skin issues like rosacea, eczema, or acne

- Mind and mood issues like anxiety, depression, ADHD, or ADD

Let's take a closer look at some of the leaky gut syndrome symptoms:

Inflammatory Bowel Disease. Hungarian researchers have found that heightened gut permeability has connections to the colon in people suffering from ulcerative colitis or irritable bowel syndrome. In another study concerning patients of Crohn's disease, leaky gut prevails in most cases and even up to 10-20% of their healthier relatives. This suggests that leaky gut could be genetic. In these cases, supplementing with zinc is effective at closing up the tight junctions of the intestines.

Food Sensitivities. People with food sensitivities may blame leaky gut for their condition. Due to the toxic onslaught on the blood, the immunity of individuals with intestinal hyper-permeability work overtime to produce antibodies, which makes their bodies susceptible to certain foods' (especially dairy and gluten) antigens.

Thyroid Problems. Hashimoto's disease is an autoimmune disease that leaky gut syndrome can affect. The disorder, also called 'chronic thyroiditis,' can lead to impaired metabolism, hypothyroidism, fatigue, depression, weight gain, fatigue, and many other concerns.

Inflammatory Skin Conditions. The skin-gut connection theory, proposed more than 70 years ago, described how leaky gut could cause skin conditions like psoriasis and acne. Medical professionals prescribe drugs and creams for skin disorders, yet you can simply fix them by healing your gut.

Autoimmune Disease. The key to knowing how leaky gut can lead to autoimmune disease is research done on the zonulin protein. Eating gluten can trigger extra-intestinal and intestinal autoimmune, neoplastic, and inflammatory disorders.

Researchers of the University of Maryland School Of Medicine found that gluten 'activates *zonulin* and leads to heightened macromolecules intestinal permeability.'

Malabsorption. Various leaky gut nutritional deficiencies include magnesium, Vitamin B12, and vital enzymes that help in digestion. People with leaky gut should supplement with a multi-vitamin based on whole foods. They should also take live probiotics to help digest their food, and ensure they get proper nutrition.

Mood Issues. In a Neuro Endocrinology Letters study, leaky gut can cause certain neurocognitive disorders. For example, intestinal hyper-permeability triggers the release of depression-inducing chemicals like pro-inflammatory cytokines.

CHAPTER 2

THE ROLE OF INFLAMMATION AND THE IMMUNE SYSTEM: WHAT YOU NEED TO KNOW

P eople often do not realize how important the gut bacteria is for our health and how crucial of the role it plays for the immune system to effectively fight infections, viruses, bacteria, toxins and other pathogens flooding our body every day.

What is the immune system?

The immune system is a complex network of organs, tissues, and cells that serves as the body's natural defense system against potential threats. These threats include fungus, parasites, viruses, and bacteria that have one thing in common – they can all make you sick. They are everywhere and you cannot escape them. The best thing you can do to protect yourself from those invaders is to boost your immune system to guard and fight your health when the threat arises.

How does the immune system protect our body?

When the body detects a potential threat, your immune system produces proteins, chemicals, and white blood cells to fight off and destroy the threat before it reproduces and causes serious damages.

As the invaders multiply, your immune system works overtime in producing the right chemicals to protect your body. As long as the immune system is healthy and working properly, you'll be protected from various health problems ranging from common colds to cancer.

What Happens When Your Immune System Isn't Working as It Should?

Our immune system is the key to proper digestion, optimal levels of energy, beautiful radiant skin and good functioning of all the organs.

However, if we constantly expose our bodies to toxins, chronic stress, commercial high carb western diet, antibiotics and poor lifestyle habits (such as overeating, alcohol overconsumption, lack of exercise, poor quality of sleep, too much pressure and tension, etc.), the immune system gets overwhelmed and collapses. When the immune system gets worn out, toxins, viruses, and bacteria overwhelm the body and we get sick.

When the immune system breaks down and identifies a safe substance as harmful, we get an allergic reaction to the substance, which we've never been allergic to before. Some of the most common substances that the immune system recognizes as threats even, when they aren't threats, include pet dander and pollen.

What is Systemic Inflammation?

Systemic inflammation is a condition in which the body is

frequently or constantly in the state of alertness. This usually manifests itself in the form of:

- musculoskeletal pain such as: back pain, neck pain, abdominal pain

- weight gain

- constant fatigue

- frequent infections

- insomnia

- depression

- anxiety

- mood disorders

- rashes

- swelling

Under normal circumstances, inflammation is alright, as it helps us to fight infections, however, chronic inflammation is detrimental for all our wellbeing.

Why does chronic inflammation affect the body?

It happens due to various reasons, the most common of which are:

- A metabolic syndrome

- Untreated chronic infections and injuries

- Long-term exposure to chemicals, irritants, polluted air and water

- Obesity and poor fitness

- Smoking

- Mild autoimmune disease

- Aging also causes inflammation. It can happen to anyone no matter how calm, skinny or fit you are. It happens as you age but some people experience it earlier than others, specifically those who have an unhealthy lifestyle. It is an indication that the immune system is gradually getting weaker.

- Chronic severe stress is another reason of inflammation and therefore it should always be our priority to address it, as no diet or supplements will be effective if there's an ongoing tension in our body, resulting in excess production of free radicals.

The Importance of the Immune System in Fighting Leaky Gut

To function well, the immune system needs the presence of probiotic bacteria which fight off threats and protect us from all kinds of infections.

Probiotics enhance the production of organic acids that lower the large intestine's PH. By doing so, they are able to prevent the growth of harmful bacteria and the metabolism of bile acids and cholesterol in the colon. This is an important factor in the prevention of cancer in the different organs in the body including the GI tract.

There are more than 100 trillion live microorganisms in the gut, which determine gut health. They make up more than 80 percent of the body's immune system. These microorganisms regulate mucosal immune system - the surfaces of the body that come in contact with external threats such as the lungs and the intestines - and metabolism. They also shield the body from infection and promote normal function of the gastrointestinal tract (GI).

The GI remains protected and its barrier intact as long as the immune system is strong due to the presence of these microorganisms. The opposite will happen when a problem is encountered by the composition of the community of microorganisms in the body known as the *microbiota*, not only the body's defense system will get weaker but it can also result in a leaky gut. This condition doesn't only compromise the health of your gut but can also cause other diseases, such as depression, chronic fatigue syndrome, obesity, and breast cancer.

Your gut health is the foundation of your overall wellbeing since having an unhealthy gut equates to an unhealthy immune system. The latter will make you vulnerable to autoimmune diseases, inflammation, and infections.

The intestinal wall of t human body is held in tight junctions. It allows micronutrients from the food you eat to go back and forth in the wall until they get through the bloodstream and become absorbed by the body.

There are many aspects in life that may cause the wall to suffer from gaps that will allow the partially digested food to go straight into the bloodstream. These aspects include chronic stress, unhealthy lifestyle, and poor dietary choices.

We will discuss all of those factors later in the book, as they are the foundation of a natural healing process.

The Huge Impact of Chronic Stress

Stress benefits the body because it alerts you to do something before an accident happens. However, it becomes a problem when you experience stressors with frequency and at high intensity. When it happens all the time, the nervous system fails to activate the relaxation response when needed. The condition becomes chronic and this is when your health starts deteriorating, if left untreated.

When you are affected by the condition, your body stays in the state of physiological "arousal" – which involves inflammation - and it affects your whole system directly and indirectly.

The human body can easily cope with acute stress, which is temporary, but the opposite is true when it comes to chronic stress. It can create havoc in your overall health.

Chronic stress is a result of unhealthy lifestyle, loneliness, high-pressure job, inability to deal with emotions, and many more. When you experience stress all the time, your natural fight or flight response to any threat or stressor is impaired. As a result, you become weary, ill, and physically and emotionally drained. It is a long-term condition that wears down the immune system, which can lead to other health problems including leaky gut syndrome,

IBS, Candida overgrowth, Celiac Disease, depression, Crohn's disease, heart ailment, and stroke.

Obesity and Inflammation

A strong and healthy immune system supports weight loss. However, when you have excess fat around your abdominal area, the body's defense system might turn against you, making you vulnerable to heart ailment and other diseases.

Various kinds of cells make up the immune system. These cells that protect the body from threats and viruses need to co-exist and maintain a certain balance to secure your health. When the balance is compromised, the cells will cause harm instead of protecting your system. The usual causes of an imbalanced immune system include excess body fat and unhealthy diet.

Excess body fat, especially in the abdominal area, leads to the creation of pro-inflammatory immune cells that lead to inflammation in the body once they get distributed in the blood. This kind of inflammation has been linked to various health problems, which include coronary heart disease. There are also inflammatory immune cells that grow within the fat tissue, known as macrophages.

Foods that Cause Inflammation in the GI Tract

An inflamed GI tract equals abdominal pain, cramping, diarrhea, discomfort, bloating, and gas. All of those symptoms can further lead to leaky gut and other digestive problems.

Stay away from the following foods to ensure the health of your gut:

Processed meat

Eating processed meat (treated with antibiotics, hormones, preservatives and fed with GMO foods) increases your risk of colon cancer, stomach cancer, diabetes, and heart disease. The most common kinds of processed meats include non-organic beef jerky, smoked meat, ham, bacon, canned meat and sausage. These meats have higher levels of AGEs or advanced glycation end products than the other meats. AGEs cause inflammation and they are formed by cooking certain foods, such as meats, at high temperatures.

High-fructose corn syrup and sugar

These two are the most common kinds of added sugar consumed in the Western diet – high-fructose corn syrup or HFCS and table sugar or sucrose. HFCS contains 55 percent of fructose and 45 percent of glucose and sucrose contains 50 percent each of fructose and glucose. These sugars increase your risk of inflammation that can cause other ailments, such as chronic kidney disease, cancer, fatty liver disease, insulin resistance, obesity, and diabetes.

Excessive alcohol

Consuming alcohol in moderation can provide health benefits but the opposite happens when you drink too much. Heavy alcohol drinkers are prone to develop leaky gut that can lead to inflammation and damage of the organs. Moderate alcohol consumption should be limited to one standard drink per day for women and two for men.

Processed fats and oils

They are alien to human body and should be avoided at all costs. They are cheap to produce and profitable for the food industry.

They are:

- Vegetable oils
- Cooking oils
- Margarines
- Butter replacements
- Spreadable butter
- Hydrogenated oils

You can find them in most processed foods such as:

- Crisps
- Snacks
- Breads
- Pastries
- Biscuits
- Cakes

- Take-away meals

- Mayonnaise

Refined carbohydrates

Unprocessed carbs from fruits, roots, and grasses are mostly healthy, rich in fiber and have been consumed by people since the ancient times. Refined carbs, however, have taken out most of the fiber and they increase the risk of inflammation. According to research, refined carbs promote the growth of the damaging gut bacteria that wreaks havoc in our body.

If you are already suffering from inflammation of the gut or you are prone to diseases related to the problem, avoid consuming the following:

- Grains and everything made of them
- Starchy vegetables
- Sugar and processed carbohydrates
- Starchy beans and peas
- Lactose
- Gluten
- Carbonated sugary beverages. They add unwanted gas into your system.
- Alcohol. If you are taking medications for your gut,

alcohol can interfere with their effects. It also prevents proper rehydration.

How to Reduce Inflammation Quickly

Hydrate your body – this will clear out the bowels, move the toxins through the kidneys and liver, and eliminate them through sweat. It will also help your body to detox from air pollution, heavy metals, pesticides, mold, and others.

Important tips for optimal hydration:

- ✓ Avoid chlorinated water. Use filtered water instead (install a reverse osmosis filter in your home).

- ✓ Begin your day with a full glass of filtered room temperature water with lemon juice, a teaspoon of high-quality vitamin C and a pinch of Himalayan salt. This drink water will absorb easily and provide your body with electrolytes supporting your nervous system throughout the day. It's a great way to flush your body from toxins. Eat your first meal min 15 minutes after.

- ✓ Drink minimum 8 glasses of clean water per day.

- ✓ Don't drink while eating. Always 15 minutes before the meal and 1,5hour-2 hours after the meal. Drinking and eating dilutes stomach acid and leads to acid reflux and digestive problems.

    Keep things moving – Exercising pumps the lymph fluid

and boosts circulation. This way you deliver oxygen and fresh blood to your tissues, which lowers inflammation by flushing away metabolic debris and providing nutrients to inflamed tissues.

Reduce stress – Pray, meditate, walk in the nature, laugh, connect with the people, journal, watch comedies, listen to jokes, practice gratefulness daily, listen to your favorite music.

Get enough of high-quality sleep – stress and lack of good sleep are your worst enemies. They increase inflammation in your body and increase the risk of serious conditions.

<u>**Tips to optimize your sleep:**</u>

✓ Go to bed by 10pm if possible

✓ Air your bedroom before you go to bed (to remove all the electromagnetic field radiation)

✓ Switch off all the electronics minimum 2 hours before going to sleep.

✓ Switch off wi-fi

✓ Do not eat proteins and fats minimum 2 hours before bed – they take a long time to digest and your digestive system instead of resetting and resting, will have to work hard overnight. As a result, you will wake up tired and drained of energy.

✓ Clear your thoughts from all the tasks that need to be done the following day. Write them down instead of cluttering your mind.

- ✓ Blackout your room or use sleeping mask

- ✓ Pray and meditate

- ✓ Practice gratefulness - think of the 3 things that happened during the day that you are most grateful for

Consider supplementing the following:

- ✓ Melatonin

- ✓ B Complex Vitamins

- ✓ Valerian Root

- ✓ Vitamin D3 (always supplement together with K2 – for improved absorption)

- ✓ Curcumin/Turmeric (supplement with Cayenne Pepper for better absorption)

- ✓ Glutathione (regulates all anti-oxidants in our body)

- ✓ Omega -3 Fatty Acids (Most of the people consume too much Omega-6 fats and are deficient in Omega-3 fats. This imbalance increases the inflammation. The recommended ratio of Omega-6 to Omega-3 should be 4:1)

Keep these plants in your bedroom:

- ✓ Aloe Vera

- ✓ Peace Lily

- ✓ Lavender

- ✓ Spider plant

✓ Jasmine

✓ Rosemary

These plants have strong purifying properties and can even remove benzene and formaldehyde from the air. They balance the levels of CO_2 and induce proper sleep.

Testing for Intolerances and Allergies

Before planning on what to eat to heal and improve gut health, you have to be certain that you are not allergic or intolerant to certain foods. Food intolerance and allergy are often confused. If you are uncertain about your condition, it is best to seek professional help before trying out experimental remedies. You need to undergo tests depending on your doctor's findings based on your family's related medical history and symptoms.

Some of the most popular tests done to determine intolerance and allergies include:

Blood tests

Radio Allergo Sorb ent Test or RAST is a specific immunoglobulin E or IgE test on a suspect food in your blood to determine the amount of IgE antibodies it has. It measures the response of your immune system to particular foods. It is more efficient to get this done in by a hospital clinician or a general practitioner. Your blood sample will be sent to a medical laboratory so that it can be tested further according to the foods that you have taken.

Skin prick test

The test is done under medical supervision. A small amount of the food you're suspected to be allergic to will be diluted and placed on the skin of your back or forearm. The skin will then be pricked using a needle so that the substance from the diluted allergen can get through the skin. If you're allergic to it, the area of the skin pricked will form a swollen lump. Testing positive in this test isn't enough to conclude food allergy or intolerance. Your doctor will perform other tests to be certain before making a diagnosis.

Elimination diet

This is also called food exclusion and reintroduction. It is important that you get this done under the supervision of a registered dietician. This way, your nutritional intake can be monitored during the testing period, especially when you are not allowed to eat major food groups.

When you undergo the elimination diet, you can't consume the suspected foods or food groups for a period of time. You will record your observations on whether or not your symptoms improved after you stopped eating certain foods. You will then reintroduce the foods and record if the symptoms return. The process helps in pinpointing suspected foods but it cannot determine whether you are allergic or intolerant. This may also not be a safe method if you experienced a severe reaction to a food in the past.

Oral food challenge

The test is done in your doctor's office where medical equipment is readily available and you are under medical supervision. It's the doctor's call whether you'll be blindfolded or not during the process. There are instances when it's better for the patient to be unaware of what they are eating. During the test, you'll be given small amounts of the suspected foods to eat. Your reaction and symptoms will be observed before the doctor decides whether or not you can reintroduce the food into your diet.

There are other alternative tests available for this purpose but while research and studies are still ongoing, it is best and safer to stick with the tests given by medical practitioners. Understand that inflammation happens due to many triggers. There are certain triggers that you can't do anything about, such as sickness, injury or pollution, but there are those, which you can control, like your fitness and the food you eat.

You need to know the foods that trigger your symptoms so you can avoid them. However, the good news is, that once you heal and re-balance your gut microbes, they will protect you from most of those pathogens trying to invade your organism. Keep on reading to learn more.

CHAPTER 3

18 WAYS TO HEAL LEAKY GUT, BOOST METABOLISM, AND LOSE WEIGHT

I n this chapter we will cover a variety of strategies that will help you cure leaky gut and improve your metabolism. They will also significantly increase your knowledge and awareness of certain lifestyle changes you can adapt to drastically improve your health and enjoy higher quality of life.

Optimizing a diet is a first step to heal your gut and break through the health problems you've been struggling with.

Along with the diet, we will focus on lifestyle changes and healing solutions forcing those gut bullies in your microbiota to give in.

So, let's dive into details...

Way #1. Keep Stomach Acid at Optimal Levels

The mainstream medical system is often unaware of the crucial role of stomach acid for our autoimmune system. You will often hear about people complaining about their stomachs being too acidic, but the truth is: high level of stomach acid is crucial for optimal

digestion. If your body is unable to produce enough stomach acid, it's more likely to experience microbial overgrowth.

Here's why improving stomach acid levels is so important:

- ✓ Stomach acid is critical for sterilizing any food wishing to make its way into your gut.

- ✓ Neutralizes bad bacteria.

- ✓ Breaks down protein - Stomach acid is also responsible for proteolysis, the process in which proteins are broken down into forms that can be properly absorbed by the body such as peptides and amino acids. This is because acids activate pepsin, the enzyme that the body needs to properly metabolize protein.

- ✓ Facilitates Vitamin B12 absorption - Stomach acid activates a glycoprotein called intrinsic factor. It enables the body to absorb vitamin B12, a nutrient that helps in keeping nerve and blood cells healthy.

- ✓ Stimulates Release of Bile and Digestive Enzymes - Bile acid in bile is crucial in the digestion and the body's absorption of fat and fat-soluble vitamins. Certain waste products are also eliminated from the body with the help of bile.

✓ Triggers Closing of Esophageal Sphincter - The Esophageal Sphincter connects the stomach to the esophagus and stomach acid triggers its contraction, protecting the esophageal tissue from harsh stomach acid.

✓ Activates pyloric sphincter - Stomach acid also activates the pyloric sphincter which connects the stomach to the small intestine and allows food to pass through.

What happens when you have low stomach acid?

If you have low stomach acid, your body won't be able to absorb key minerals and proteins. When this happens, you suffer from vitamin or mineral deficiency. Remember that proteins have to be properly metabolized so the body can absorb enough amino acids that are needed for vital bodily functions including recovery.

In addition, low stomach acid can also leave you vulnerable to infections. Some of the health conditions associated with low acid levels include leaky gut, chronic fatigue, malnutrition, constipation or diarrhea, gas within an hour after eating, diabetes, small intestinal bacterial overgrowth (SIBO), anemia and weakness, a variety of food sensitivities.

When the body is unable to produce enough stomach acid to break down proteins, molecules of partially digested proteins end up in the small intestine. This triggers the pancreas to release more enzymes to metabolize the proteins. If that happens occasionally, it won't be so damaging, but if this happens frequently over time, the pancreas may not be able to keep up and there will be too much stress on the intestinal lining, causing irritation. When the gut lining is irritated, leaky gut syndrome is very likely to develop, leaving the body exposed to toxins and harmful organisms.

Causes of low stomach acid

There are a number of contributing factors including poor diet and improper eating habits (eating in stress, eating on the go, overeating), chronic stress, overuse of antibiotics, zinc deficiency, H Pylori infection. Two of more common causes are stress and poor diet particularly intake of too much sugar.

What to do if you have low stomach acid levels

Improving acid level in your stomach primarily involve addressing the causes.

Here are some things you can do:

Try a low carb diet

Two of the food major food types that are linked to a weak gut lining is grains and beans, which are both high carb food. This is because the gluten in grains tends to cause an autoimmune response from the body, causing your own immune system to attack your gut. Gluten also triggers the production of a substance called zonulin which wears out the connection between cells in your intestinal walls. These two food types also have high phytic acid and lectin content, which damages the gut barrier.

Chew your food well

This may seem simple but it's actually important. Digestion starts at the mouth and eating your food too quickly can affect your body's capability to digest food. Take smaller bites and take your time when eating. Chew your food well so your saliva can play its role well in starting the digestive process.

Avoid processed food

Processed food causes inflammation in your stomach and decreases acid activity.

Eat fermented vegetables

Fermented food like kimchi and sauerkraut have probiotic effects that help keep your stomach healthy, improve digestion and reduce inflammation in your stomach. It also helps fight harmful bacteria and is linked to a healthier immune system. You'll learn more about fermented vegetables in way #4.

Eat foods that enhance digestion

Two things you can try including in your regimen are organic apple cider vinegar and ginger. A chapter of this book is dedicated to a guide that can help you transition to a gut-friendly diet especially during the first month. Apple cider vinegar is fermented liquid that is rich in enzymes that help break down bacteria in food. Don't drink pure apple cider though because it can damage your teeth in its non-diluted form. You can dilute 1-2 tablespoons in a glass of water (approximately 250ml)

Take digestive enzymes.

Make it a habit to relax your body before eating a large meal.

This will help your system in activating the parasympathetic nervous system that will boost the production of stomach acid.

SOMETHING TO KEEP IN MIND

Low stomach acid may also be a sign of low thyroid function. If you suspect this may be an issue, get your thyroid checked out.

Way #2. Apply the 4 Rs Protocol

REMOVE foods and factors that cause inflammation and damage the gut while creating the environment for overgrowth of bad bacteria, parasites and Candida.

Here's what to remove in the first place:

Gluten: Gluten is hard to digest, pierces holes in your gut lining and raises levels of gliadin and *zonulin*, which trigger intestinal permeability. The main sources are wheat, barley and rye. **The most popular gluten foods to remove include:** bread, pasta, pizza, cereal, cookies, sausages, sauces, beer, crisps, crackers, ready-made meals

Sugar and artificial sweeteners - they cause a radical shift in the gut bacteria that lead to changes in the gut microflora and metabolic outcomes

Refined Oils: Canola oil, Vegetable oil, Soybean oil, Corn oils, Safflower, Margarine (and any other 'buttery' spread)

Unsprouted Grains

Alcohol

Conventional Dairy Products

Processed foods

Tap water (contains chlorine)

NSAIDS

Antibiotics

Synthetic Food Additives. Most of the highly processed foods contain food additives that destroy your gut lining. Stay away from: cookies, crackers, chips, microwavable ready-made foods, processed meats and sausages.

Additives commonly used in the food industry that you should avoid at all cost:

Polysorbate 80

Bisphenol-A (BPA)

Bisphenol-S (BPS)

Artificial coloring

Gut-damaging habits or lifestyle choices you have to quit:

Eating too much.

Eating in stress.

Eating to 'fix' your emotional problems (eating when depressed, sad, anxious, happy, excited, etc.).

Lack of regular physical routines. Exercising doesn't have to be complex. You can do house chores, gardening, biking, or walking. The physical activities that you do help in burning energy, promoting metabolism, and improving gut health.

Smoking. Smoking causes a lot of ill effects on your health, including the gut. Giving it up can greatly improve the gut flora, which will become evident after nine weeks of quitting this bad vice.

Lack of high-quality sleep. Disruptions in your body clock caused by lack of sleep compromise your gut bacteria. This is because the gut follows the body's circadian rhythm that gets disrupted when you don't get enough sleep or you don't sleep on time.

Mismanaging stress. While you can't avoid stress, especially as you grow older, you have to learn to do effectively deal with it. Too much stress leads to the reduction of gut flora diversity. It also reduces beneficial bacteria, such as Lactobacilli, and increases harmful types, such as Clostridium.

REPLACE with healing foods.

Replace gut-destroying food with gut-healing nutritious food, which is easy to digest and supports repairing the lining of intestinal wall.

Here is What to Eat:

Bone Broth. Homemade bone broth provides vital amino acids and minerals including potassium, glycine, and proline that can improve mineral deficiencies and help heal and seal leaky gut. Bone broth is so beneficial that we dedicated an entire subsection for the bone broth cleanse (way #4).

Steamed Vegetables. Vegetables (non-starchy) that are steamed or, cooked can be digested easily and form part of the leaky gut diet.

Raw Cultured Dairy. Probiotic Yogurt, amasai, and pastured kefir, are some of the best probiotic foods supporting gut healing process. When buying yogurt, make sure that you look for the types with at least 1 billion of active or live CFUs or colony-forming units.

Fermented Vegetables. Include kvass, coconut kefir, kimchi, or sauerkraut. The probiotics in these foods work by balancing the pH levels in the small intestine. In the next section (Way #4), we will discuss fermented vegetables in detail.

Good Fats. Consume healthy fats that are easy on the gut. Include organic egg yolks, ghee, raw unsalted butter, coconut oil, and avocados.

Sprouted Seeds. Hemp seeds, chia seeds and flax seeds are the most beneficial sources of fiber which supports the growth of good bacteria. However, if you suffer with severe leaky gut, it's better to avoid them temporarily and once the condition improves, gradually introduce them back into the diet.

Raw Cacao. It is loaded with polyphenol flavanols that have prebiotic and heart-healthy effects. Making it a habit to drink it every day will reduce the bad bacteria and increase the good bacteria in the gut.

Omega-3 Fatty Acids. Wild-caught salmon, organic lamb, grass-fed beef will be the best sources of anti-inflammatory sources of Omega-3 Fatty Acids.

REPAIR with gut-health promoting supplements

Introducing supplements will help you digest food better. As a result, your body will absorb more nutrients necessary to heal your gut. Supplements will also nourish your intestinal lining and create environment supporting and feeding good bacteria that fight with toxins coming with food, air, water, etc.

Here are the supplements that will support your healing:

L-Glutamine (search for pure, unflavored, highly-absorbable)

Digestive Enzymes (choose the ones without binders, fillers, gluten or GMO)

Probiotics (look for the ones with multiple strains of bacteria)

Vitamin D3 (always take together with Vitamin K2)

Vitamin C (should be pure, highly-absorbable, made from acerola extract is one of the best ones)

Zinc – prevents undigested food particles from seeping through the gut lining and into the bloodstream, where they can trigger inflammation or autoimmune reactions. Since zinc supports the gut's mucosal lining, it is important in fending off allergic reactions, infections, and various symptoms due to gut permeability (including skin disorders, fatigue, mood changes, aches, and many more). Zinc is a natural component of foods like turkey, lamb, chicken, yogurt, pumpkin seeds, or grass-fed beef.

Magnesium (Magnesium oil body spray is very effective form of supplementing magnesium)

Deglycyrrhizinated licorice (DGL)

Activated Charcoal

Collagen peptides

Colostrum

Quercetin

Turmeric (for proper absorption, add pepper and eat with good fat)

Caprylic Acid

The omega-3 fatty acids_(buy only the ones that have high amounts EPA and DHA). Reduces inflammation, supports gut, heart, brain, and immune system. You can take fish oil daily, or you can regularly consume various fatty fish.

REBALANCE with probiotics.

Probiotics are great at keeping your gut healthy. They serve as the "lookout" in the gut lining, alerting your body so that harmful food particles and toxins cannot get into your bloodstream. As a result, you'll have lower risks of inflammation and stronger immunity functions. That's why it's crucial to take probiotics and probiotic supplements daily.

Probiotics do not only keep your gut in good shape. They are the beneficial bacteria that promote healthy gut microflora.

The microflora 'communicate' with intestinal lining's cells and 'tell' the intestines what to absorb into the blood and what to keep from passing to the body. If the 'bad' bacteria in your gut outnumber the 'good bacteria,' malabsorption – which is when harmful substances can penetrate to the blood – can happen.

Probiotics are involved in breaking down foods and turning them into nutrients.

Probiotics regulate immunity. If inflammatory bacteria overrun the good bacteria in your gut, you may develop food allergies and get sick. They can help you manage conditions such as candida and SIBO.

Your gut bacteria should ideally be abundant and diverse as such composition can lead to better gut function, turn off inflammatory signals, and numb down oxidative stress. The benefits of protective and diverse bacteria in your gut include less belly fat, better metabolism, and an easier time to lose body weight.

In a Japanese study, for example, consuming fermented milk with probiotic bacteria for 4 weeks led to a loss of belly fat by 8.2%. The waist-to-hip and body fat percentage reduced slightly.

To stay slim or lose weight, boost metabolism, and keep the gut healthy, add a few probiotic foods to your dietary regimen:

Kefir. The slightly tangy, drinkable, and smooth yogurt has a dozen varieties of active cultures. Kefir, which is 99% lactose-free, allows lactose-intolerant individuals to digest it easily. Consuming kefir in small amounts is a good way to test lactose intolerance. If you experience no symptoms, you may increase your consumption. Moreover, kefir has 8-11g of protein.

Kombucha. Kombucha is tangy, fizzy, and has a slight vinegary flavor. The SCOBY gives kombucha its natural carbonation. The SCOBY also contains the yeast and bacteria that creates the probiotics. However, you may want to know that kombucha has trace alcohol amounts, so better consume only one 12-ounce bottle daily.

Sauerkraut. There is even more reason to consume sauerkraut. The condiment made from cabbage is essentially a hotdog sandwich topping. If you want to get the best probiotics out of sauerkraut, eat fresh homemade sauerkraut. As for store-bough sauerkraut, get it from the refrigerated section or read the label to see if there are any live cultures.

Miso Paste. You may not know it, but that miso soup you eat at Japanese restaurant contains probiotics. Miso paste comes from fermented and aged soybeans. Miso paste is also rich in fiber, protein, and Vitamin K. Use miso to glaze chicken or fish before cooking, add miso to liquid and make miso broth, or add miso in a stir-fry dish.

Other fermented products that have beneficial healing properties include:

- Homemade Apple Cider Vinegar (ACV)

- Homemade yogurt

- Fermented milk

- Kimchi or spicy Asian fermented cabbage

- Lassi or the combination of fermented yogurt and milk

- Beetroot Kvass

Supporting with probiotics can help. For example, ingesting a probiotic supplement for 14 weeks significantly reduced zonulin and led to less oxidative stress in men who trained after an intense workout.

How to add probiotics to your daily regimen:

- Each day, consume a probiotic food, using them as a snack or condiment. Kefir, kombucha, sauerkraut, and miso are good examples of probiotic-rich foods. Especially beneficial and widely available is yogurt (high quality). Other foods rich in probiotics are kimchi and fermented vegetables.

- Aside from fermented foods, you can get probiotics in capsule, powder, and tablet forms, all of which contain the dried form of bacteria. You can also opt to take fermented dairy products, such as milk drinks and yogurt, for their live probiotic culture content.

- If you are too busy to remember to take gut-friendly supplements, you can opt to include them in your everyday meals. Make it a habit to stock up on fermented vegetables in the fridge. Aside from being tasty, they also have a long shelf life and convenient because you can eat them without cooking. They make perfect side dishes or you can use them to add flavors to your favorite dishes.

- It is better to make your own fermented vegetables than buy them at stores. You have to be certain that they don't contain added sugar and preservatives and have gone through the right preservation process. You'll learn more about fermented vegetables on the next page.

- If you find it hard or don't have the tools to make them, then choose to take supplements to supply your body with probiotics each day. It is also important to know that two probiotic strain supplements counteract inflammation and promote diversity. The Bifidobacterium strain enhances immune function and helps to inhibit potentially harmful pathogen growth. The lactobacillus strain converts sugars and lactose into lactic acid, which helps the gut to produce an adverse environment for harmful bacteria.

- In choosing probiotic products, it is recommended to look for the kind with at least 1 billion CFU and contain some of the most researched types, such as Saccharomyces boulardii, Bifidobacterium, and Lactobacillus. Choose the product with at least 15 different strains and known for its strength. Look out for store brands that have not gone through proper testing for strength and effectiveness.

- Finally, keep in mind that probiotics are not recommended for people with a weak immune system. If you suffer from the condition, you can ask your doctor's advice about the best probiotics that will not compromise your health.

It is normal to experience gas, changes in the stool pattern, and bloating when taking probiotics. They indicate that they are working. You may not easily find the right probiotics for you but don't easily give up. Try different products until you find the kinds that will work for you.

Way #3. Include Fermented Foods and Veggies into Your Diet

Fermented foods are probiotic. Naturally fermented foods are effective in making your gut microbiome stronger. The process of fermentation extends not only the shelf life of the food but also its nutritional content. Eating fermented foods supply your system with live microorganisms, healthy probiotics that aid in the digestion process.

It's important to eat naturally fermented foods in order to benefit from them. Most of the fermented foods available in the groceries did not go through the natural fermentation method if using live organisms but were pickled using vinegar. The latter does not contain probiotics.

If you can't make your own, look for specialty stores with fermented foods that contain the tag – naturally fermented. You will know that a jar of fermented food has live microorganisms when you see bubbles in the liquid after opening the jar.

Fermented foods are rich in beneficial bacteria that help in preventing digestive issues and other concerns, such as leaky gut syndrome, gut dysbiosis, and candida. Your body has natural stores of healthy gut bacteria but they get destroyed through time due to poor lifestyle and wrong choices of food. Fermented and other probiotic-rich foods replenish the healthy gut bacteria in the body. The fermentation process also makes the food easier to digest.

If you are not used to eating fermented foods, especially fermented vegetables, it is best to gradually introduce them into your system. You can add them to soups and other dishes. When adding fermented veggies to soups, wait until it is slightly cool before stirring the fermented food because too much heat kills the good probiotic bacteria.

How to do it

Here's an ideal way to introduce this kind of food into your everyday diet:

Option A.

1. Start with the classic and the most common – cabbages or sauerkraut. Mix the juice of homemade sauerkraut to broth or soup. Cabbage contains lots of fiber so it is best to discard them while you are still getting used to the effects of eating fermented food. Add up to 2 teaspoons of the juice to 1 cup of meat broth or soup.

2. When your body has adjusted and doesn't show any negative response, you can begin adding 1 teaspoon of sauerkraut cabbage to your every meal.

3. Increase the amount of juice and cabbage through the days and begin trying other types of homemade vegetables.

Option B.

Actually, you can ferment almost any kind of vegetable but the best ones are

- Carrots

- broccoli

- peppers

- cabbages

- radishes

- beets

- cauliflower

- asparagus

- whole pickling cucumbers

It's just that some vegetables need a little more care than others. Some processes may vary as well. To illustrate, leafy greens such as cabbages don't need a lot of water so you won't need much brine for fermentation. This is because they have high water content and will just create their own brine if you put enough salt. There are also vegetables such as cucumbers and squash that could get mushy during fermentation so you might want to add high-tannin ingredients such as grape leaves in order to keep them intact.

Tips for successful fermentation

Try to make slices as uniform in size as possible. Of course, it's impossible to make every slice exactly the same but you can at least try to make sure that they're roughly the same size. This way, they'll ferment at around the same rate.

Keep it anaerobic with salt brine. The key to fermentation is that it happens when your main ingredient is not exposed to oxygen.

Otherwise, there'll be mold growth and you don't want that. Cover your vegetables in salt water.

You will need to release the gasses, so choose a container with a breathable lid or just open the jar for a few minutes every few days to let air out.

You can use cheesecloth or paper coffee filters. If you feel it's wasteful, try a reusable coffee filter that fits your jar well.

Store your fermented vegetables in a cool place such as the fridge or the root cellar. That way, your supply will keep well for months.

Taste your fermented foods every once in a while. It's okay to open that jar and have a taste. You can make adjustments to the taste if you want.

Use clean equipment. You can even sterilize the jar to make sure no bad bacteria will ruin your ferments. Otherwise, clean your equipment with gentle soap and rinse with hot water.

Pack the jar up to 80% full. Try not to let too much air in your jar because that can lead to mold and yeast growth. Add more ingredients or brine and if that isn't possible, choose a smaller jar.

Signs of Bad fermentation

So how do you know you shouldn't even try tasting because the batch has gone bad?

Here are the signs to look out for:

- ✓ It's moldy. This is signified by a pink, black, blue or unusual blue green coloration or a fuzzy appearance.
- ✓ It has a repellent smell. Note that fermented food does smell

sour but you'll know it's bad when it's no longer sour but putrid.

✓ Your stomach is upset. Let's say you weren't sure if a batch is bad and you tried it anyway, you know it's not a good idea to keep eating them when you end up with an upset stomach.

One of the most popular ways to ferment vegetables is to make sauerkraut. It is also the easiest to prepare, taking only about 15-30 minutes. Essentially, you just need to pack all ingredients in a clean jar, then allow them to ferment for 3-10 days.

Here is a simple probiotic-rich recipe for Classic Sauerkraut:

Classic Sauerkraut

Yields: 1 ½ quarts

Ingredients:

- 3 lbs. green and/or red cabbage
- 1 ½ Tbsp. sea salt

Method:

Rinse the cabbage and discard any withered or bruised outer leaves. Slice in half across the core. Then, slice into thin strips with a sharp knife. Alternatively, slice the cabbage halves into larger chunks and shred in the food processor.

Place the shredded cabbage into a large bowl and sprinkle in the salt. Massage the salt into the cabbage until the liquids start to get drawn out of the leaves. Continue to massage and squeeze to draw out as much water as possible.

Stuff the shredded cabbage into a clean jar along with the liquids. Press down on the cabbage to make sure that the leaves are completely submerged in the liquids. There should be an inch of space between the rim and the mixture. Cover the jar with a cheesecloth secured with rubber bands.

Place the sauerkraut in a cool shelf away from direct sunlight, with a temperature approximately between 50 and 75 degrees F.

Allow the sauerkraut to ferment from three to nine days, checking once every other day by checking the smell and taste. Always pack down firmly on the shredded cabbage to keep them completely submerged.

Once you are satisfied with the flavor of the sauerkraut, transfer the jar into the refrigerator and refrigerate for up to 6 months.

Tips to make your first perfect fermented veggies:

- Use only hard heads of fresh cabbage.
- Do not rinse the cabbage. Rinsing will remove the microbes.
- Use vegetables with higher sugar content in smaller quantities to prevent yeast or slimy brine. It can even make the ferment more alcoholic.

If you are using finely-chopped apple, do not ferment it too long. Sugar in this fruit speeds up the process of fermentation.

Troubleshooting

If the cabbage turns pink during the process, discard the section where the color appeared. The change of color is an indication that you used too much salt, you applied it unevenly, or the cabbage is not completely covered by the brine.

If your fermented food does not have enough tang or sweetness, let it ferment for several days then taste it again.

If it is too salty, add a raw potato slice to absorb the excess salt to the dishes. You can also rinse it before consumption.

Way #4. Do the 3-Day Bone Broth Cleanse

The bone broth challenge is similar to water fast. You'll consume liquids throughout the day while taking a break from eating solid foods. Instead of water and herbal tea, you will consume 5 to 8 cups of bone broth per day. It is challenging but offers lots of health benefits that include restful sleep, clearer skin, faster metabolism, improved digestion, and increased energy.

Its main advantage over water or dry fast is that it promotes the consistent intake of protein, electrolytes, and essential nutrients. Its goal is to sustain your energy, prevent dehydration, and satisfy your appetite. The concept combines the beneficial effects of intermittent fasting and drinking bone broth.

Benefits of a bone broth cleanse

This cleansing method offers a wide range of benefits, which include the following:

- It boosts your energy and gives you more passion to continue doing what you love.
- It helps in slowing down the aging process.
- It makes you feel better and younger.
- It heals and prevents inflammation.
- It heals the digestive system.
- It makes the nails healthier and it adds thickness and shine to your hair.

- It helps in making the skin firmer by boosting its elasticity. It prevents free-radical damage and other signs of skin aging.

- It makes your overall complexion naturally plumped and radiant.

- It makes you healthier in general.

- It heals and prevents leaky gut.

Bone broth is naturally satiating so you don't have to worry about hunger. It is sugar-free so taking it for 3 days will starve the bad bacteria in your digestive system. Since it is easy to digest, you can take it even if you have a sensitive stomach or you are suffering from Celiac disease.

The challenge is to consume around six 8-ounce cups of broth every day for 3 days. The broth contains Glycine, its main amino acid, which your liver will use to perform the detoxification process. You can adjust your intake of broth depending on how your body is responding to it. As a caution for people with high blood pressure, it is important to always monitor your sodium intake. You can consume more bone broth per day if you can. If you think that you require more hydration but don't want to add more broth, you can instead drink a few cups of water.

The end of the 3-day cleansing program is crucial. You have to continue eating the right foods and introduce your system to fermented foods, organic vegetables, and other sources of probiotics important for your gut health.

How to Do It:

The first step towards a 3-day bone broth cleanse is preparation.

Here are the steps to get this done:

1. Start with a 12-hour mini-fast and don't jump into a full 24-hour fast on your first day. You have to help your system get used to the process. It is also important to choose the right schedule. Instead of starting the fast at the start of the day, you will start after your last dinner at 7 PM. This way, you won't feel hungry at the start of your fast and it also won't affect your sleep.

2. As the fasting lasts, it is only natural for your system to feel hungry. It is still not used to functioning without solid foods. Embrace the feeling and complain if you must, but make sure that you don't break the fast.

3. Surround yourself with a strong support group. You have to explain to your family what you are doing and why. If they understand your goal, they can support you throughout your ordeal by making it easier for you to stick to the plan.

4. Buy the right ingredients and gather important tools needed to make and stock up the broth you'll need throughout the cleansing phase and even the following days after.

It is important to choose bones from grass-fed, pastured, and organic animals. They come from animals exposed to only a few toxins with healthier and nutrient-dense bones. As much as possible, choose bones with a lot of cartilage because it contains collagen that breaks into gelatin.

Here are some of the best types of bones:

- Neck bones
- Calf's foot
- Beef marrow, feet, joints, and knuckles bones
- Chicken feet
- Full turkey or chicken carcass
- Meaty bones, such as short ribs, shank, and oxtail
- Chicken wings and thighs
- Pig's foot
- Head and bones of a wild-caught fish

Tools needed for the process:

- Stockpot
- Slow cooker
- Small mason jars
- Fine-mesh strainer

5. You will consume approximately 1 gallon of bone broth for 3 days. You need to consume five to six 8-ounce cups of bone broth, plus 64 ounces of water throughout each day for 3 days.

6. On the fourth day, you will reintroduce your system to a healthy diet. You will eat probiotic foods and vegetables and consume three 8-ounce cups of bone broth, plus 96 ounces of water throughout the day.

Here are a few simple recipes to get you started. There are more in recipe section further in the book.

BONE BROTH RECIPES YOU CAN MAKE AT HOME

Gut-Healing Chicken Bone Broth

Yield: 12 cups

Ingredients:

- 3 celery stalks (rinsed and chopped)
- 2 onions (roughly chopped)
- 1 large carrot (rinsed and chopped)
- 3 bay leaves
- 1 1/2 cups apple cider vinegar
- 1/2 cup fresh flat-leaf parsley
- 1/2 tablespoon black peppercorns
- 2 1/2 pounds chicken necks and backs
- 2 1/2 pounds chicken wings

- Sea salt to taste

- 1 1/2 pounds chicken feet

Method:

1. Put the meat in a stockpot. Add enough cold filtered water to cover all the ingredients. Set the heat to high, cover the pot, and leave to boil.

2. Loosen the cover and reduce heat to medium. Leave to simmer for 1 hour. Periodically check the broth and discard the foam that rises on the surface.

3. Reduce heat to low while keeping the pot's cover loose. Simmer for an hour. Add the celery, onion, carrot, peppercorns, parsley, bay leaves, and apple cider vinegar. Mix all ingredients and leave to simmer for a couple of hours.

4. Remove from heat and allow to cool slightly.

5. Scoop out the solid ingredients from the broth. Strain the soup using a fine mesh strainer and season it with salt. Leave until completely cooled. Transfer to small jars, close the lids and freeze. The broth will last for a week in the fridge and up to 6 months in the freezer.

Turkey Bone Broth

Yield: 5 quarts

Ingredients:

- 7 quarts filtered water

- 2 bay leaves

- 1 mandarin orange peel (or lemon/orange peel)

- 1 small bunch of parsley

- Turkey giblets

- 1 carcass from a roasted turkey

- 6 garlic cloves (smashed)

- 1 large onion (chopped)

Method:

1. Put the meat in a stockpot over medium-high flame. Add onion, bay leaves, orange peel, parsley, and garlic. Add enough cold water to cover all ingredients. Bring to a boil. Reduce heat to medium-low and leave to simmer for 10 hours.

2. Discard the solid particles and use a fine-mesh strainer to strain the broth into a big container. Ladle it into jars and leave to cool.

3. Scoop out the fat at the surface of each jar. Cover the jars and keep in the fridge or freezer.

Thai-Flavored Pork Bone Broth

Yield: 12 cups

Ingredients:

- 2 teaspoons sea salt

- Cold filtered water

- 3 tablespoons cider vinegar

- 1 yellow onion (chopped)

- 2 pounds pork bones (rinsed)

- 1 head of garlic (smashed)

- 4 ribs celery (chopped)

- 2 inches fresh ginger (chopped)

- 4 scallions, chopped (instead of the yellow onion)

- 1 large daikon radish (roughly chopped)

- 1 fresh lemongrass stalk (remove the outer layer and chop)

Method:

1. Put the meat into the pot. Add apple cider vinegar and enough water to cover all the ingredients. Leave for 30 minutes.

2. Add the rest of the ingredients and gently stir. Cook on high flame for 20 minutes. Reduce heat to low once the liquid starts to boil. Loosely cover the pot and simmer for at least 6 hours or up to 24 hours. Periodically check the soup and discard the foam that settles on top.

3. Remove solid ingredients and strain the soup into small jars. Leave to cool. Store in the fridge or freezer.

Slow Cooker Beef Bone Broth

Yield: 12 cups

Ingredients:

- 2 tablespoons apple cider vinegar
- 1 bay leaf
- 3 celery stalks
- 4 pounds mixed beef bones marrow bones, short rib, knuckles, oxtail, etc.
- Cold filtered water
- 2 medium carrots
- 2 medium onions

Method:

1. Arrange the mixed bones on a baking tray in a single layer. Roast in a preheated oven at 400 degrees for 30 minutes. Turn over all the pieces of mixed bones and roast for 30 more minutes.

2. Prepare the veggies by chopping the celery, onions, and carrots. Place them all on a crockpot. Add the roasted bones, bay leaf, and apple cider vinegar. Add enough water to cover all ingredients. Cover the pot and cook for 24 hours at a low-temperature setting. Periodically check to remove the foam on top. Add water, if needed, to keep the ingredients submerged in it while cooking.

3. Remove the solid particles and strain broth using a fine-mesh

strainer. Leave to cool and transfer to small jars. Refrigerate for 2 hours. Discard the fat that settles on top of each jar. Cover the jars and store in the fridge or freezer. The broth will stay fresh for a week in the fridge and up to 3 months in the freezer.

Nutritious Fish Bone Broth

Yield: 10 cups

Ingredients:

- 3 bay leaves
- 1 lemon (quartered)
- 1 cup white wine vinegar
- 1/4 cup fresh flat-leaf parsley
- 6 1/2 pounds wild-caught fish heads and bones
- 2 1/2 tablespoons olive oil
- 1/2 tablespoon black peppercorns
- Sea salt to taste
- 3 celery stalks (rinsed and chopped)
- 2 fennel bulbs (roughly chopped)
- 2 onions (peeled and roughly chopped)

Method:

1. Clean the fish by rinsing, removing the gills from the head, and rinsing the bones. Set aside.

2. Heat olive oil in a stockpot over high flame. Sauté onion, celery, and fennel until warmed. Reduce heat to low and continue cooking until the vegetables are tender.

3. Set the heat to medium. Add the white wine vinegar and leave to simmer for several minutes. Add the fish bones, lemon, peppercorns, bay leaves, and parsley. Pour enough cold filtered in the pot to cover all ingredients. Set the heat to high, cover the pot, and bring to a boil.

4. Reduce heat to low, loosen the cover, and leave to simmer for 1 hour and 30 minutes. Periodically check the broth and scoop out the foam that rises on top. Remove from heat and allow to cool.

5. Remove the solid particles and strain broth using a fine-mesh strainer. Season with salt and leave until completely cooled. Transfer to jars, cover, and store in the fridge up to 5 days or up to 6 months in the freezer.

Way #5. Consume Resistant Starch

Resistant starch – an example of which is potato starch – helps with weight loss and promotes healthy gut flora. Resistant starch is a kind of fiber that you cannot digest, but your intestinal flora can. It resists breakdown in the small intestine and stomach and enters the large intestine intact. Once in the large intestine, the starch acts as your gut flora's food. The bacteria in your gut ferment the resistant starch into short-chain fatty acids.

You are likely to eat resistant starch from two sources. The first type occurs naturally in raw food like green bananas and raw potatoes. Other sources include peas, oats, and corn. The second type of resistant starch comes in the form of cooked and cooled foods. For example, cooked potatoes that have been cooled have resistant starch. Another example is cooked and cooled rice.

How to Do It

Consume foods with resistant starch. You can also supplement with 20-30g of potato starch (unmodified).

The apparent link between gut health and resistant starch is the gut flora. Aside from providing food for the gut flora, resistant starch can make probiotics effective by protecting bacteria while they make their way to the gut. The starch also ferments in the colon. Theoretically, fueling the large intestine cells keeps them healthier, improves the gut health, and reduces colon cancer risk.

Way #6. Maintain Acid-Alkaline Balance

First things first, let's talk pH. PH levels refer to the acidity or alkalinity of a substance. It's a scale that ranges from 1 to 14, with 7 being the middle point used to indicate neutral acidity/alkalinity. A pH level above 7 means that the substance is alkaline, while levels below 7 indicate acidity.

Your body performs a delicate balancing act been acidic and alkaline pH, but it's difficult to maintain and the body uses up a lot of energy just to do it. There are factors that can disrupt this balance including stress, toxins and certain chemicals, as well as lifestyle choices. Note how eating drastically changes your stomach acids pH levels. The pH level of your stomach level increases when you eat and then go back down to normal after digestion. This is again because the body performs this natural balancing act.

When we talk about the acid-alkaline balance though, we're not just alluding to your digestive system although what you eat plays a role in this balance as well. The balance we're referring to is your body's overall pH levels which start at the bloodstream.

Keep in mind that your circulatory system is involved in delivering nutrients to your body which means that it plays a role in cell repair, reducing inflammation, and maintaining energy levels. The acid-alkaline balance is also responsible for clearing toxins. The body needs to get rid of excess acid, which is the waste product of doing normal body functions.

Blood pH levels must be between 7.25 and 7.45 and if that balance is disrupted, your body won't be able to function properly. Your body sends energy to restore balance and to compensate for excess acid, your body will even tap into vitamin and mineral reserves in your tissues including bones, teeth, and organs.

Maintaining an acid-alkaline balance in the body therefore helps speed up recovery from injury and helps ensure that your cells have energy for various body functions.

How to maintain acid-alkaline balance

1. To help your system achieve the balance it is aiming for, you have to implement the principle of correct food combining. Different foods get digested at different rates, so it will help to group foods and eating or not eating them together to promote optimal digestion. Eat fruit before and not after a meal and avoid combining protein and starches in the same meal. Carbs need an alkaline environment and protein needs an acidic environment to be broken down. It is best to eat fruit on an empty stomach for better digestion.

2. Avoid eating eat acidic and carb-loaded food at the same meal. Different enzymes in the body deal with the digestion of protein and carbs. Eating them at the same time will cause digestive problems and for the partially digested food to stay in the gut while waiting for their turn to get digested. The waiting period is crucial since the food in the gut has a high chance of fermenting or getting rotten and can cause diarrhea, constipation, or gas.

3. Note that the goal is not to completely go alkaline – the goal is to

strike a balance. The 80/20 rule is the general recommendation to meet this goal. 80% of your diet should be alkaline forming foods and the rest could be acidic food. However, everybody is different so feel free to tweak your acid/alkaline ratio depending on how your body reacts. If you are too acidic, see the list below to find out what you should be eating and avoiding.

Highly Alkaline Foods - Raw spinach, raw broccoli, brussels sprouts, cauliflower, carrots, cucumbers, asparagus, artichokes, olive oil, raw zucchini, blueberries, collards, avocados, bananas,

Neutral pH – most tap water, unsalted butter

Somewhat Acidic Foods PH – Milk, Yogurt, fruit juices, sugar, chicken and turkey, canned fruit, white rice, salmon, tuna, tea, cooked spinach, kidney beans

Very Acidic Foods PH Sodas, lamb, pork shellfish, wine, cheese, vinegar, many processed food

4. One of the things that could throw your balance off is stress. That's why a significant aspect of living a life with acid/alkaline balance involved managing stress, which we will discuss in detail in the following section.

Way #7. Limit Medications

While antibiotics eliminate bacteria (even those good bacteria in your gut), prescription medication for anxiety, pain, and blood pressure management can interfere with digestion, causing acid reflux or heartburn. Do not go wrong by taking another drug to counteract this. Consult with your physician and see if there is any other way to prevent prescription drugs from triggering gut issues.

Limit your medications to the essentials, so they do not interfere with gut activity.

Also, monitor your vitamin D levels. Low levels of vitamin D in the body are linked to poor gut health. Moreover, medications can deplete vitamin D supply and other vital nutrients.

Also, avoid NSAIDs and ibuprofen. Since they are anti-inflammatories, they can damage your gut's function. A big no-no is to take ibuprofen and then work out or train vigorously.

NSAIDs can damage the intestines' protective barrier and restrict flow of blood to the kidneys. A relatively recent study exhibits how NSAIDs can damage such bodily functions. Several male study participants took 800mg ibuprofen and then did cycle training. Testing after working out showed that the men developed intestinal injury. Researchers then determined that using NSAIDs can harm gut health and must be discouraged.

How to Do It

Instead of NSAIDs, take natural remedies like Boswellia and

curcumin as both of them have anti-inflammatory attributes known to promote the gut's health. Boswellia, for example, does not restrict flow of blood to the kidneys. It also lowers inflammation by targeting Cox 1 and 2 pathways as ibuprofen.

Derived from turmeric, curcumin lowers muscle pain after a hard workout, as curcumin can minimize inflammation. It is also determined to improve the function of the gut in children having irritable bowel syndrome.

Way #8. Identify and Avoid Food Intolerances

Food allergy or intolerance happens when a particular food leads to permeability of the cell layer that protects your body. If you cannot tolerate gluten, for instance, consuming foods with gluten will cause your body to produce zonulin, which can cause the tight intestinal junctions to open up and lead to leaky gut.

Zonulin – in the right amounts – is not harmful per se. It enables the absorption of nutrients into your body. However, intolerances to food can cause your body to produce excess zonulin, which can break down the intestinal junctions and allow potentially harmful substances to enter the bloodstream. This may lead to an immune response.

Aside from gluten, other foods that cause intolerances include tree nuts, peanuts, lactose, shellfish, soy, and eggs. Moreover, you may even get food intolerances from coffee or strawberries. People with weak intestines risk random intolerances more since their gut has been leaking bodily substances for a time.

How to Do It

Try eliminating wheat and gluten from your diet and determine if there are any positive changes. If you are still experiencing gut issues, you may have to stop eating other foods as well, or you may need to take an extreme way to heal your gut.

You may also take food allergy tests, including an IGE

(immunoglobulin E) test or an IGG (immunoglobulin) test. The IGE test measures food allergies that are severe, whereas the IGG test measures for food intolerances that are milder.

Aside from gluten and wheat, certain foods create imbalance in the gut. They also create candida and intestinal inflammation.

It is best to avoid as much as possible the food items below:

- **Cow Dairy.** A1 casein, which is a cow dairy-based protein, can lead to a reaction similar to gluten. Moreover, the A1 casein can be 26 times more harmful than gluten.

- **Gluten.** A diet without gluten can improve leaky gut symptoms. The sticky protein – gluten – resides in grain products like wheat, and it is difficult to digest unless it has passed through a sprouting or sourdough process.

- **Un-Sprouted Grains**. Soy and grains – when unfermented and un-sprouted – have phytic acid, which may irritate the intestines.

- **Sugar.** Sugar feeds bacteria and yeast that could damage the intestinal wall. If you want to use a sweetener, you can use local honey (raw). Bear in mind though that you should consume natural sweeteners sparingly.

Way #9. Exercise

Training too hard can lead to inflammation that can damage the gut's tight junctions if you do not effectively recover. Any kind of stress, including mental stress, intense training, and sleep deprivation all raise cortisol levels. High cortisol levels boost the release of histamine, which is a compound that speeds up the immune system. If a stressful life or a lack of recovery from working out raises cortisol, your immunity activates chronically, until stress kicks in and you fall ill.

Histamine raises the secretion of gastric acid, which leads to bloating and the release of substances that affect the tight intestinal junctions and make the gut leak. Histamine also triggers neurotransmitters, which raise stress response and stimulate the nervous system.

Elevated histamine's major symptoms include red or itchy skin, bloating, poor endurance, and poor motor performance. If you recover well after training and eat right, exercise encourages gut health.

How to Do It

If your life is stressful, try to do 2 to 4 intense strength training workouts (lasting no more than one hour) weekly. However, you must focus on recovery – sleep, nutrition, deep breathing, and hydration. If your lifestyle is calmer, you can benefit from workouts that are more frequent. However, ensure exercise does not become a chore. If you do workouts twice daily, do them for shorter periods.

Whatever your case is, it is important to take care of yourself and your gut. Avoid drugs, and get plenty of fiber, probiotics, and other gut-friendly food. You may also want to try some relaxation exercises to help heal your gut, and help you lose weight.

Hip Extension. This is excellent for the nervous system, particularly if you are exercising intermittently or have not done proper exercises in a while.

- With your arms at the sides, lie down on your back. Bend your knees and feet flat on the floor.

- Lift your hips gradually off the floor by squeezing your buttocks. Push your heels on the ground.

- Ensure that your knees align with your ankles and hips. Do not flare inward or outward. Gradually drop your hips down to the floor.

- If you feel pressure on your lower back, squeeze together your buttocks before starting the exercise.

Prone Cobra. This exercise increases mobility in and opens up the thoracic spine. It can also raise your energy levels.

- With arms at the sides, lie facing down.

- Breathe deeply and slowly. As you inhale, lift your chest from the floor while squeezing together your shoulder blades. Rotate your arms so your thumbs point up and your palms face away from your body.

- Align your neck and head. Do not tilt back your head and keep your toes on the floor. Keep this position until you need to exhale. Do it slowly while gradually lowering your chest back to the ground.

- If you feel stress on your lower back, squeeze together your buttocks before starting the move.

Wood Chop. This exercise can increase intra-abdominal pressure to stimulate digestion. It can also relieve stress.

- Stand straight with your arms at the sides.

- Inhale and – with hands together – bring up your arms over your head.

- Exhale and bring down your arms. Bend at the waist in the same manner as if you cut wood with an ax.

- When your move naturally ends, pause for a moment before you go back to your standing pose.

- You can change up your chopping motion to the left, center, or right.

Depending on your state of health or physical condition, the exercises may seem extremely challenging or easy. In any way, they can still enable your body to heal your gut.

Way #10. Soothe Yourself with Essential Oils

Some of the best essential oils to take for leaky gut are ginger, fennel, and peppermint. Many people worldwide deal with digestive issues including chronic illnesses like inflammatory bowel disease, leaky gut, and acid reflux. Moreover, acute issues like cramps, bloating, constipation, and diarrhea affect almost everyone at some point.

As Hippocrates says, "All health begins in the gut." Leaky gut and other digestive issues can cause the development of problems like thyroid issues, food intolerances, skin issues, fatigue, and – over time – autoimmune disease.

Fortunately, an essential oil blend contains peppermint, ginger, coriander, fennel, tarragon, anise, and caraway that may support digestion. This blend can:

- Reduce nausea.

- Support healing leaky gut.

- Act as an anti-inflammatory.

- Improve acid reflux.

- Treat constipation, diarrhea, and IBS.

- Reduce cramps.

- Freshen breath.

GINGER ESSENTIAL OIL. It is an anti-inflammatory oil and can help settle gastrointestinal distress. Using ginger oil can also strengthen immunity and help heal leaky gut. Ginger also reduces anxiety, slows aging, and benefits joint health.

FENNEL ESSENTIAL OIL. This oil has a sweet natural flavor and can help relieve indigestion and a host of other stomach issues. It can also reduce stomach cramps, and treat colic and cough. Fennel also helps get rid of toxins by naturally balancing hormones and stimulating the liver.

PEPPERMINT OIL. It can soothe the digestive tract and can cool gut inflammation. This oil effectively improves circulation and benefits acid reflux. Moreover, peppermint oil can reduce nausea symptoms.

How to Do It

- Diffuse in the air to reduce sensation of nausea.

- Place 3 to 5 drops in water and take three times a day to improve digestion.

- Place 3 drops under the tongue to relieve stomachache.

- Massage 2 drops of oil clockwise over the belly to reduce constipation and bloating.

- Place 3 drops in mouth before taking meals to reduce acid reflux.

- Mix with baking soda and coconut oil for a homemade toothpaste.

Way #11. Calm Your Mind

Stress is tied to the gut, and the body responds to stress through 'fight or flight,' related to cortisol levels and ruled by the hypothalamic-pituitary-adrenal axis. If you are in a temporarily stressful situation, your body's systems can easily go back to normal. If you have chronic stress, however, your body stays in that fight-or-flight state for longer periods.

What is critical is that the body does not always distinguish mental from physical stress. Thus, your body would respond similarly if you encounter a bear and if you realize you dislike your job. The body will fight stress in the same way. Ongoing stress can cause chronic inflammation; the body considers stress as an infection and attempts to overcome it.

Since inflammation is at the core of many diseases, such prolonged exposure to stress can seriously affect your health, with diseases ranging from autoimmune disorders to high blood pressure. The 'good bacteria' in the gut are crucial to how immunity responses regulate.

Moreover, the gut microbiome relates to disorders like autism and depression. Health care experts and researchers, for years, have noticed people with autism often have GI issues like gluten intolerance and food allergies. This made researchers to think that there may be a connection about autistic individuals' gut makeup.

Thus, stress is always at the root of leaky gut syndrome, and the best way to deal with it is to cut it out of your life and work as much as possible.

How to Do It

- Remove those email apps from your smartphone.

- Use an email blocking app on your desktop or laptop like Freedom or Self Control to ensure you do not check emails outside of working hours.

- During your lunch hour, go out and walk for 20 minutes while doing deep breathing exercises. Slowly eat your lunch and then rest for a while. You may also do a light and quick gym session, followed by a short sauna and a brief yet slow lunch.

- Try to listen to soothing music throughout the day. For example, if you look at a high-stress office environment (a Wall Street investment bank's open floor plan), you will see that most of the analysts wear noise-cancelling headsets. You can drown out stress and the noise.

- With your co-workers, set expectations. If you assert yourself and be reasonable, you can still get your point across.

- When you reach home, do some destressing. You can use 20 minutes to breathe, stretch, or write down what is in your head. You will notice stress slipping away.

Way #12. Remove toxic chemicals from your household

You have to be smart about the products and chemicals that you bring into your home. Many countries do not implement strict rules in the chemical composition of commercial products. The responsibility of eliminating toxic products from your home is now in your hands. Many of these products contain carcinogenic ingredients that cause various health concerns, including behavioral disorder, infertility, and cancer.

Toxins can lead to leaky gut, and toxins damage your digestive system more as they get through the gut barrier and into the bloodstream. The obvious first step to eliminating toxins is not taking them in your drugs, drinks, or food. However, it is also worth investing in products that help decrease toxins that may enter your body.

How to Do It

Have a shower head filter fitted. The filter keeps chlorine at bay. Chlorine can be toxic and its vapors from your hot showers can directly hit the body.

Have your dwelling tested for mold. Hidden mold can do a lot of damage to the body in the end, and leaky gut syndrome is a casualty of the mold menace.

Use organic personal care products. These include shampoo, toothpaste, and body wash, among other skin care items.

Convention supermarket products can contain various chemicals that should not enter your body's system, let alone enter your gut barrier and your bloodstream. Switch to organic products and lower the toxic load.

Use air filter. This may be necessary if you live in a sufficiently polluted city.

Instead of buying chemical-loaded cleaners, try mixing your own cleaning supplies. You can try natural ingredients as cleaning agents or try mixing two lemon juice, baking soda, and vinegar. You can also opt to buy organic cleaning products now available at specialty shops. They may be more expensive than the usual commercial products but are safer and free from toxins.

Avoid using plastic. While it is still impossible for a home to become plastic-free, which largely depends on where you live and your lifestyle, you can implement radical changes to at least limit your use of plastics. They are non-biodegradable and toxic chemicals were emitted during their production. They are toxic not only to people's health but also to the environment. You start by carrying your own reusable bag when you shop, refrain from using plastic straws and other materials, such as coffee mug, cutlery, plate, and water bottle.

Before buying any kinds of skin care products, check the Environmental Working Group's Skin Deep database. This will give you an idea of what certain products contain and how the ingredients can affect your skin and health. The database has more than 60,000 products listing. As you get informed about the toxic chemicals of the products, you can apply the information when buying your cosmetics and avoid buying and using the types that can harm your skin.

Open your windows. This is to allow fresh air to flush out the smell of toxic chemicals in your home.

Avoid using non-stick pans. The surface of the cookware is filled with chemicals called poly and perfluoroalkyl. These substances can cause various health problems, such as developmental issues, damage to the organs, thyroid disease, and infertility. It is better to use cast iron and other non-coated cookware.

Way #13. Get Adequate Sleep

Daily stress and poor sleep may be the more important issues to address when you need to heal your gut, aside from dealing with food allergies and intolerances. After all, lack of sleep and poor nutrition can increase oxidative stress.

Moreover, the combination of bad sleep and stress alters hormone and neurotransmitter levels, which makes you act in ways that do not help the gut: you can make poor diet choices, you do not chew your food well, and you turn away from protein and whole plants and consume high-carbohydrate foods. You may also be less active and such bodily behavior can reduce good gut bacteria.

How to Do It

Fix your circadian rhythm and get a good night's sleep. This promotes sleep by optimizing overall health and hormone balance.

Sleep depends on what you do during the day. Thus, you should integrate light exercise, take a Vitamin D supplement, or soak in the sun during the mornings. Also, do not drink a lot of caffeine.

You may need to cut back on certain unnecessary activities, which is a way to make time for sufficient sleep. You may cut television time down to 20 minutes a day, completely avoid weekly social dinners, or read books for only a maximum of 1 hour a day. Such activity changes can free up time and help you sleep for 8 to 9 hours.

Way #14. Detoxify your body

Since it is inevitable to get exposed to toxins and other harmful chemicals not only from the products you use but also from the food you eat and environmental pollutants, you have to give your body its well-deserved pampering on a regular basis by detoxifying.

The detoxification process gets rid of the toxins in your body. It aids your organs that handle your body's natural detoxification methods, such as kidney, skin, and liver, by taking the pressure off them, giving them a break, and in the process, make them healthier.

The process is crucial for weight loss and overall health. It helps in keeping you on track of your body weight and sets you up to develop healthy habits to ensure that you won't lose sight of your fitness goals. Aside from helping your body organs get rid of most of the toxins in your body, the process also helps in boosting your immune system and in keeping you healthy and strong.

General Tips

The detoxification process doesn't have to be complex. There are three simple techniques that you can do every day anywhere you are.

1. **Drink lots of fluids.** Consume at least 4 liters of water each day to help in flushing out the toxins inside your system. Aside from removing impurities, drinking plenty of water also boost your energy, aids in the weight loss process, and makes your skin healthier and clearer.

2. **Go organic with the food you eat.** Refrain from eating anything sprayed with pesticides. Choose healthy foods as well and avoid consuming refined, processed, and packaged foods. You must also limit your consumption of sugar, salt, and oil.

3. **Exercise.** It makes you sweat, which is a good way to eliminate toxins from your body. It will also keep you fit and strong.

4. **Go to a sauna.** You can go to a spa, or you can invest in your own personal sauna. While you cannot eliminate all toxins, sweating in a relatively mild sauna for 30 to 45 minutes may work to aid the body's natural detox process.

5. **Make a Coffee Enema**

There are indeed many ways to get this done but one of the most effective ways is through a coffee enema. This alternative healing method is used in cleansing the colon. A mixture comprised of water and brewed and caffeinated coffee is inserted in the colon through the rectum. It boosts the bile flow and gives instant relief to people who are suffering from constipation.

Linda L. Isaacs, M.D., an alternative medicine physician, wrote in an article that anyone can benefit from coffee enemas since people are constantly exposed to pollutants and toxic chemicals in water, air, and food. The process helps by stimulating the liver to discard the harmful elements inside the body.

The process must be taken with caution. Make sure that you are guided accordingly if you are going to do it. It can cause an electrolyte imbalance and bacterial infection if administered improperly. You can go through the process if you are taking medicines that interact with caffeine and if you are sensitive to caffeine. If not done right, a coffee enema may cause bowel perforation, bloating, vomiting, nausea, rectal burns, infection caused by unsterilized equipment, dehydration, and cramping.

The process can be done at home but make sure that you have been checked by a doctor, you have all the necessary tools, and you know all the important information needed to get it done. While the second option is more expensive, it will be safer to get the process done in a holistic health clinic. It is crucial to drink plenty of water after undergoing the process in order to prevent dehydration.

How to Prepare a Coffee Enema

Prepare the ingredients and tools needed for the process:

- Organic coffee (Use only the best organic coffee)
- Filtered water
- Rolling enema hose clamp
- Rubber colon tube
- 1 quart or 5-quart glass enema bucket kit
- Quart mason jars or half gallon mason jars
- Coffee enema filter
- Beaucoup paper towels
- Lubricant of choice

- Non-toxic disinfectant

- Squatty Potty

- Poo-pourri spray

- Intimate equipment soap

- Witch hazel

Here are the steps to prepare a coffee enema:

1. Make the coffee mixture. Put a liter of boiled filtered water, plus 2 tablespoons of organic coffee in a glass French press. Leave for 5 minutes to steep before pressing. Allow to cool for 2 to 3 hours.

2. For the enema container, you can use a glass bucket or stainless-steel bucket with a clamp or 2-quart enema bag. Remove air from the enema tube and close the clamp. Pour the coffee mixture in a clean enema bucket. The mixture has to be lukewarm. It will be painful if it's too hot and you will have a hard time holding your Caboose Coolatta if the mixture is too cold. Apply a lubricant at the tip of the enema.

3. Lay down of your left side. Hang the filled enema bag with the clamp closed 1 foot above your tummy.

4. Gently insert the enema tip into your backside until you have inserted about 12 inches. It should not be painful or uncomfortable. You will feel a little resistance each time you get past a sphincter and you need to get past through 2 of them. Once inserted, you can

now open the clamp while holding the enema bag 1 foot above your tummy. Get your hand ready near the clamp. After a few seconds, the liquid will begin to flow. Close the hose clamp if you develop a cramp. Take deep breaths and turn from side to side. Begin again once the cramp is gone. You can regulate the flow of the coffee by squeezing the hose with your fingers.

5. Once the liquid is inside the colon, slowly pull the tube while allowing its end hang in a sanitized container. Begin your timer for 12 minutes. Turn to your other side and make sure you're completely relaxed. Before the end of the timer, roll again to your left side.

6. Go to the toilet and discharge the enema. You can stay a little longer in the toilet to make sure that all the liquid has been released. Make sure that you do not push. Allow the liquid to naturally get out while you relax.

7. Reheat the remaining coffee, if necessary, and repeat the steps while holding the liquid inside your colon for 15 minutes.

You will need the other materials in cleaning up the materials once you are done.

Troubleshooting Guide

Here are some tips about what to do in case you encounter any of these problems:

1. **Tasting coffee in the mouth.** Relax and don't worry because it is a common occurrence since the process triggers a flavor sensation.

2. **Blood in the stool.** This may be an indication that you have removed or inserted the tube from your backside in haste. Soothe the affected area by dabbing coconut oil and allow it to completely heal before repeating the process.

3. **Unexplainable stuff in the poop.** Since this is unusual, it is best to consult a doctor when it happens, especially when you can't identify what the strange stuff is.

Way #15. Keep Candida and SIBO under Control

SIBO (Small Intestinal Bacterial Overgrowth)

SIBO is essentially a growth of bacteria in the wrong place, and such bacteria can be either good or bad. It happens as a result of bacterial overgrowth in the small intestine when they are supposed to grow in the gut. As a result, the bacteria use up your stored nutrients and leads to malnutrition. Its symptoms, which mainly affect your gut, include the following:

- Indigestion

- Constipation

- Diarrhea

- Cramps

- Bloating

- Stomach pain after eating

- Weight loss

- Gas

- Feeling full often

It is still unclear what causes SIBO but it is believed that it happens due to an underlying health problem. You'll be at high risk of suffering from SIBO when your GI tract is compromised. It is curable but may happen again and again. If left untreated, it can cause malnutrition and dehydration.

Treatment

The condition can be treated through proper diet and antibiotics. Incorporating probiotics to your diet helps minimize SIBO symptoms. Drinking plenty of filtered water (non-chlorinated) also helps reduce plain and improves digestion.

Candida Overgrowth

Candida, on the other hand, can be an unwelcome and horrid leaky gut syndrome symptom, which is when the intestinal lining becomes inflamed and irritated that it can no longer function properly. The compromised intestinal lining then starts to 'leak' bacteria, food particles, yeast, and other toxins into the blood. Your immune system then fights such toxins, leading your immunity to exhaust itself. You then become vulnerable to infections like candida.

The human body contains the candida fungus in small amounts. Despite the presence of candida, people remain healthy, as the small concentration of candida is not enough to lead to infection. However, if the gut balanced is disturbed, the candida fungus takes advantage of the imbalance and overrun certain digestive tract areas.

People who have an imbalanced gut flora and weak immune system have a high risk of encountering problems with this yeast. The immune system helps in controlling the yeast's overgrowth but once it gets out of control, the condition will trigger different symptoms that include the following:

- Asthma or eczema flare-ups

- Hives, itching, skin rashes

- Confusion, frequent mood change, headaches

- Joint pain

- Repeated oral or vaginal thrush

- Abdominal pain, diarrhea, indigestion, gas, bloating, and other IBS symptoms

More often than not, candida overgrowth occurs at the same time with leaky gut. Candida yeasts release zymosan and other toxins that initiate inflammation all over the body. The inflammation aggravates leaky gut and causes more damages to the gut lining.

Causes of Candida

Having increased levels of stress hormones in the system elevates your blood sugar levels and suppresses the immune system – two factors that cause candida overgrowth.

Many types of antibiotics are broad acting and kill off not only the offending yeasts in the system but also the friendly bacteria in the gut. It is recommended to take a probiotic during and after taking antibiotics in order to replenish the good bacteria in the gut.

Eating too much refined carbs and sugar feeds the bad bacteria and can lead to candida overgrowth.

Taking an oral contraceptive pill that contain oestrogen, can also increase your risk of candida overgrowth.

Treatment

There are three steps to treat candida:

Step#1. Stop the overgrowth.

Step #2. Make sure you have good levels of friendly bacteria.

Step #3. Apply effective ways to heal the gut (these steps apply to SIBO as well).

Step #1. Stop the yeast overgrowth.

- Begin with a detoxification fast.

- Eliminate sugar (processed carbs as well) from your diet.

- Switch to a low-carb diet.

- Take a supplement, caprylic acid, which pokes holes in the wall of the yeast and eventually kills it.

- Take antifungal medication to speed up the process.

Step #2. Rebuild your system's stores of good bacteria.

This step will keep the yeast's population under control. Use probiotics to repopulate your gut with good bacteria. Take anti-fungal herbs and natural supplements.

Step #3. Heal your gut.

Eat a diet that doesn't feed yeast in the gut. This includes foods low in sugar and refined carbohydrates. Eat foods rich in fiber, as it feeds the good bacteria.

Consult with a functional medicine doctor and remove antibiotics, steroids, or hormones - unless absolutely medically necessary.

Way #16. Try Intermittent Fasting (IF)

Eating on time and on a regular basis may be a habit but it doesn't mean that it is the natural process. Intermittent fasting (IF) adapted the lifestyle of people who lived during the caveman days. They hunt for food and managed to survive without eating for a period of time while they were still searching for food. The gut bacteria need enough time to rest and repair. It can only do so if you will stop eating for a period of time. The process helps in preventing diseases and reducing inflammation.

There are two types of IF – short-term and long-term.
Among the two, the short-term IF will be better in healing the gut. It increases the diversity of gut microbiota and reduces gut inflammation. IF, in general, is also beneficial for gut repair.

Short-term IF allows you to eat during the hours included in your eating window.

The common types of short-term intermittent fasting include:
The 12-hour IF. You will eat three meals each day. You can decide on the time when you will start the fast. For example, you have to

schedule your eating window from 6 AM to 6 PM and fast from 6 PM to 6 AM the following day. You will break the fast with a light breakfast.

The 16-hour IF. You will still choose the schedule of your fasting period that will last for 16 hours each day. Most people who follow this program skip breakfast and schedule their eating window from 11 AM to 7 PM. This is recommended for people who frequent the gym to lose fat and build muscles. Women are typically advised to limit the fasting period to 14 hours per day.

The Warrior Diet. Fasting happens for 20 hours each day and you'll break the fast by eating a large meal at night. The fasting period is not that strict. You are still allowed to snack on a small serving of fruit or vegetable, so it is more of under-eating than not eating at all. You will then overeat during the 4 hours of your eating window.

The 16-hour diet is the most popular among the three types of short-term IF. Since your body is already in a fasting mode while you're asleep, it is easier to wait for a few hours upon waking up to eat your first meal.

While doing any kinds of intermittent fasting, you are still allowed to consume water and coffee or tea with no sugar or creamer in.

Best Methods and tips to do intermittent fasting:

Allow your body to adjust.

Start slow and give your body a chance to get the hang of the changes before committing to the plan.

Ask your doctor if you are qualified to fast and there are no serious contraindications. Especially if you are taking medications, follow a special diet programs or experience any of those:

- ✓ Recently underwent a surgery

- ✓ Pregnant women and breastfeeding mothers

- ✓ Have an eating disorder

- ✓ Malnourished or underweight

- ✓ Recuperating from fever

- ✓ Have serious mental health concerns

    Diabetics

Plan your fasting schedule during the hours when you'd mostly be asleep. This will make it easier for you to avoid temptations and thwart your cravings.

Keep yourself hydrated.

Especially during the fasting hours when you are awake. It will help in keeping you feeling full and will make it easier for you to stick with the plan.

Choose the kind of exercises that will not trigger a hunger response.

It is important to continue exercises even while fasting so that your body won't feel drained and tired. Listen to your body when you exercise and stop when it tells you that it has had enough.

Carefully plan your meals.

So that you don't get to eat the same thing over and over again during your eating window. This will make you look forward to the hours when you can eat after successfully accomplishing a fasting phase.

Way #17. Eat Good Fats and Eliminate Bad Fats

Cleaning up your diet by using the right fats and oils is essential to restoring your health from the inside out.

Quick facts about fats:

- ✓ Every membrane of every cell in our body is made of fat.

- ✓ Our brain is about 60% saturated fat.

- ✓ Healing fats provide building blocks for cell membranes and hormones.

- ✓ Fat is needed in the absorption of fat-soluble vitamins A, D, E, K, D.

- ✓ Fat is needed to aid in absorption of minerals

- ✓ Animal fats have nothing to do with arteriosclerosis, heart disease and cancer.

- ✓ Processed fats, hydrogenated fats and cooking vegetable oils cause heart disease, arteriosclerosis and cancer.

Good fats

Saturated animal fats are good fats that are heart-protective, enhance the immune system and are essential for our body to properly utilize omega-3 and omega-6 fatty acids.

We need saturated, monounsaturated and polyunsaturated fats to be healthy.

By the way, did you know that human breast milk is 48% saturated fat, 33% monounsaturated and 16% polyunsaturated? Mother nature knew what she was doing as babies grow beautifully when breastfed. Nature doesn't make bad fats, factories do.

Include these saturated fats in your gut-healing diet (use them for cooking):

*Organic, virgin and pasture-raised forms are the best

- Butter
- Ghee
- Tallow
- Chicken fat (schmaltz)
- Duck fat
- Lamb fat
- Coconut oil
- MCT oil
- Eggs
- Seafood (sardines, wild caught salmon - great sources of Omega-3 fatty-acids)
- Meat
- Grass-Fed Dairy

Include these unsaturated fats in your gut-healing diet (use uncooked):

*Organic, extra virgin or cold-pressed forms are the best

- Olive oil

- Avocado oil

- Olives

- Avocado

- Pecan/Walnut/Macadamia Oil

- Nuts and Seeds

- Nut and Seed Butter

Bad fats

In this group we have extremely unhealthy processed fats and oils that are highly toxic, pro-inflammatory and contribute to a series of diseases.

Fats to avoid:

- Canola oil (aka Rapeseed Oils)

- Vegetable Oil

- Rice Bran Oil

- Soybean

- Corn oil

- Margarine

- Cottonseed oil

- Grapeseed oil

- Peanut oil

Way #18. Include Digestive Enzymes into Your Diet

Enzymes are extremely important for breaking down carbohydrates, protein and fats and prepare them for proper digestion and assimilation in the body.

People who experience leaky gut syndrome, Candida overgrowth and other digestive issues, are often unable to produce sufficient amounts of digestive enzymes to properly digest food they are eating and assimilate all the nutrients, vitamins and minerals needed to stay healthy.

Poor digestion results in more inflammation in the gut lining, which then contributes to leaky gut syndrome.

It is key to provide digestive system with a wide spectrum of enzymes, as they play important role in out body:

- Reduce inflammation in the gut
- Reduce allergies and food sensitivities
- Support healthy microbiome balance
- Improve digestion and assimilation of the nutrients
- Improve skin and tissue healing
- Reduce stress on the digestive system

The most important enzymes for digestion improvement include:

- ✓ Amylase
- ✓ Glucoamylase
- ✓ Lactase
- ✓ Lipase
- ✓ Papain
- ✓ Invertase
- ✓ Pectinase
- ✓ Phytase
- ✓ Xylanase
- ✓ Proteolytic enzymes
- ✓ Bromelain
- ✓ Protease
- ✓ Peptidase

When choosing the right digestive enzyme supplement, remember about few things:

- ✓ The supplement should consist of wide variety of enzymes (breaking down carbs, protein and fat, lactose, and fiber).
- ✓ Stomach pH and intestinal pH differ significantly – a good supplement should function in a wide pH range.
- ✓ As intestinal stress is a major culprit to the formation of the

leaky gut syndrome, it is best to find bioavailable enzymes that reduce the stress on the intestines on the gut and improve the nutrient absorption.

✓ A good broad-spectrum digestive enzyme formula should contain lipase, protease, papain, lactase, alpha-galactosidase, hemicellulose and other enzymes.

Enzymes typically come in a capsule form.

You can swallow the capsules or mix them with your food or drink and consume at the start of your meal. This will give enough time for the enzymes to break down the food in your stomach before it goes to your small intestine.

If you opted to swallow the capsules, it will take a longer time before the coating gets dissolved inside your system so that the enzymes could start working on your food.

You can get the capsules either in gelatin-based or vegetable-based kind. They will both dissolve in the gut but most people say the gelatin-based capsules dissolve faster.

Enzymes also come in the form of enterically coated tablets that you cannot open and have to wait until the coating gets dissolved in the intestines before they could act on your food.

When buying enzymes, you have to check the dosing on their labels and how many capsules each pack contains. You also have to make sure that they don't contain fillers, gluten, and additives.

Aside from digestion, these enzymes offer other health benefits depending on the dosing.

Consuming proteases in between meals give "non-digestive" healing benefits, which include the following:

- Migraines

- Fibromyalgia

- Arthritis

- Bruise

- Detoxification

- Blood cleansing

You can also ask a doctor or research on your own about the dosing necessary for the enzymes to treat autoimmune conditions.

Healing time depends on the condition you are trying to treat using the enzymes. Gut healing typically lasts between six to eighteen18 months if the condition is severe.

Suggested Dosing

- For overall health maintenance and general digestion – follow the dosing on the product's package

- Gradually introduce a broad-spectrum enzyme in your food until you reach the goal of taking 1 capsule at your every meal.

- You will then slowly add a strong protease enzyme in your food until you can take a capsule at your every meal.

- If you are still not taking a probiotic, start taking them between or at the end of your meals.

- Your next goal is to take a yeast-targeting enzyme capsule between your meals until you are taking 1 capsule thrice each day.

- Take a yeast killer along with the yeast targeting enzyme at each meal.

It is better to go gradual about the process but if you think that your body can handle more, then you can opt to speed up the process.

For people suffering from yeast problem, bad bacteria, very poor digestion, and injured gut, it is recommended to choose broad-spectrum enzymes without high proteases content and take the high protease product separately.

Try the GAPS Diet

The Gaps Diet is extremely powerful in healing all gut-related conditions. My gut-healing story has started with this diet and helped me a lot with fixing my digestive problems.

The Gaps Diet aims to take care of your gut and in doing so helps you lose and maintain your optimal weight, cope with mental problems such as depression and anxiety, and address the digestive disorders resulting from eating unhealthy foods and poor lifestyle habits.

Here is what you should know about this diet:

The GAPS diet plan is divided into stages.

Stage 1. It sets the foundation of gut health. At this stage, you'll eat mostly soup, broth, and probiotics. You have to be gradual about the process of eliminating foods that your system is already accustomed to.

Here's a list of foods that you can eat at this stage:

- Cooked vegetables –boy choy, cauliflower without stalks, broccoli without stalks, carrots, collard greens, peeled eggplant, garlic, ginger root, kale, onion, fresh pumpkin, summer squash, winter squash, spinach, turnips, zucchini

- Boiled meats and seafood or simmered in water or broth – beef, chicken, lamb, quail, turkey, duck, wild-caught fish

- Fats – animal fat (chicken), tallow

- Herbs and spices – sea salt

- Sweeteners – raw honey

- Ferments – 1 teaspoon of fermented vegetable juice mixed with your meals, homemade yogurt fermented for 24 hours or more

- Beverages – mint tea, ginger tea, chamomile tea

Stage 2. You can now eat eggs, casseroles, stews, fermented fish, and homemade ghee. Gradually introduce egg by adding one egg yolk to 1 cup of meat stock or soup. Observe how your body responds to the egg until you can take an egg yolk for each serving of soup per day. Once done, you can add soft boiled eggs to the soup and observe how your body is reacting to the food.

You can continue eating the foods included in the first stage, plus the following:

- Poultry – organic or pastured raw egg yolk

- Fruits – avocado

- Fats – ghee, coconut oil

Stage 3. You can now increase the amount of probiotics foods that you mix with your soup or meat stock. You can now eat fermented vegetables, including the cabbage in the sauerkraut. You can start taking supplements but wait and observe how your system responds with it before making it part of your daily routine. You can eat food items from the previous stages, plus the following:

- Cooked vegetables – celery, cabbage, asparagus

- Fats – Raw or sprouted nut butter

- Herbs and spices – Cooked fresh herbs.

- Fermented vegetables – sauerkraut

- Flour – maximum of 1/4 cup each day of coconut flour or almond flour

Stage 4. You will introduce juicing at this stage. You will also add the following from your food list:

- Extra virgin olive oil

- Grilled and roasted meats

- Dried herbs

- Carrot juice

Stage 5. You can now start eating raw vegetables drizzled with olive oil. You can also start eating fruits, but most people include them after 6 months into the diet in order to control Candida overgrowth. If you want to eat fruits, start with pureed apples and cranberries. You can also try juicing other vegetables aside from carrots, such as mint leaves, celery, and lettuce. You can also add the following in your food list:

- Peeled raw vegetables

- Mangoes

- Tomatoes

- Homemade pear and apple sauce

- Vegetable juicing (organic vegetable)

Stage 6. It is now allowed to start consuming honey and raw fruits.

Here's a list of foods you can add from what you can eat:

- Fruits – raspberries, pineapple, pears, peaches, kiwi, dates, cherries, banana, berries, raw apple

- Coconut

- Coconut milk

The GAPS Full Diet.

At this point, the results of the many months that you have spent following the diet will be more evident. Aside from weight loss, you will feel better since you are eating mostly healthy foods, you will become more alert, and will have fewer instances of getting sick.

CHAPTER 4

LIFESTYLE CHANGES SUPPORTING HEALING LEAKY GUT SYNDROME

H opefully, your leaky gut has healed once you've applied all the tips and suggestions from this book. If not, don't worry. Stay consistent and add some more lifestyle changes that will support you in your pursuit to regaining perfect health and energy. Do what you can, but never come back to old unhealthy lifestyle and bad eating habits.

AVOID TOXINS. Aside from environmental factors, you can usually get them from personal care products with too many chemicals, tap water, conventional meats, and unnecessary drugs.

GET A GOOD FILTERING DEVICE FOR YOUR WATER. Tap water contains fluoride and chlorine, which become toxins once they enter your body and get distributed in the bloodstream.

DRINK HEALTHY AND CLEAN LIQUIDS, SUCH AS WATER AND HERBAL TEAS, 90 PERCENT OF THE TIME. You can occasionally consume coffee or wine but take them in moderation.

BE KIND TO YOURSELF. It is alright to ease up every once in a while. For example, you can devote 6 days in a week doing healthy habits, such as exercising, meditating, and getting at least 8 hours of sleep and then allow yourself some leeway for 1 day – stay up late, eat something sinful. But be sure to get back to healthy habits the next day.

If you have an addictive personality and you want to avoid temptation altogether, just be forgiving to yourself when you do lapse and then just get back to your gut-friendly habits with renewed energy.

TAKE PROBIOTICS, DIGESTIVE ENZYMES, L-GLUTAMINE, FISH AND KRILL OIL ON A DAILY BASIS.

GET MOVING IN THE WAY YOU LIKE BEST AND DO IT EVERY DAY. Exercise but be aware of your limits. Excessive heavy weight lifting and cardio can cause stress in the body, especially in your central nervous system. Stress is one of the major causes of leaky gut.

WATCH OUT FOR YOUR STRESS TRIGGERS TO PROTECT YOURSELF. Establish boundaries and learn when it's time to take a step back and take care of yourself.

LEARN TO SAY NO WHEN YOU HAVE TOO MUCH ON YOUR PLATE. This one is crucial if, like me, you are addicted to food. Overeating, even if it's the healthiest superfood in the world, will always be bad for your gut health.

TAKE A HIGH-QUALITY MULTIVITAMIN EVERY DAY, especially when you are recovering from a leaky gut. It makes up for the nutrients that you lack in your diet. It also boosts nutrient absorption, which has become impaired once you have developed a leaky gut. Make sure the multivitamin has no fillers and binders that would further compromise your digestive health.

AVOID EATING FOODS LOADED WITH ARTIFICIAL FLAVORING AND PRESERVATIVES. Have a healthy snack if you experience cravings throughout the day. Walnuts, raw dark chocolate, coconut oil, avocado or grapefruit are my choices.

NO PROCESSED FOODS- AT ALL.

CHECK THE LABELS AND LOOK UP THE NUTRITIONAL VALUE. Buy the most natural and unprocessed foods you can afford. Of course, organic and pasture-raised option are the best when it comes to meat, eggs, butter, vegetable and fruit.

FIND A GOOD HOLISTIC DOCTOR. Watch your health to detect related conditions early on.

STOP USING PROCESSED VEGETABLES IN COOKING AND AS AN ADDED INGREDIENT TO FOODS. As we've said earlier, industrial vegetable oils, such as sesame oil, sunflower oil, safflower oil, peanut oil, grapeseed oil, canola oil, cottonseed oil, soybean oil, and corn oil, contain high amounts of omega 6s. These oils are prone to oxidation once cooked, which can lead to inflammation and other diseases. Use quality fats for your food, such as lard, ghee, and coconut oil, which taste great and hold a high smoke point.

SAVOR THE PROCESS OF DRINKING AND EATING. Follow Gandhi's principle of chewing your drink and drinking your food. It is recommended to chew your food up to 20 times but you can increase the count up to 30 or more if you are eating something tough. This way, your gut won't be bombarded with large chunks of undigested food and it will be able to process food easier.

GO ORGANIC. While it is a bit more expensive, you will reap the benefits of eating organic vegetables, meats, and fish over time. They are free from toxins and organic fish and meats are rich in omega 3s needed to cure inflammation caused by a leaky

ELIMINATE OR LIMIT YOUR COFFEE INTAKE TO ONLY A ONE CUP PER DAY. Drink only organic coffee as inorganic has been treated with pesticides and fertilizers and bleached. You can replace coffee with healthier and gut-friendly drinks, like green tea, white tea or herbal teas.

GET INFORMED ABOUT DRUGS AND OTHER MEDICATIONS THAT COMPROMISE GUT HEALTH. Aside from doing your own research, it is better if you could ask advice from your doctor about the unnecessary drugs that contribute to imbalances in the gut flora and leaky gut. Learn how not to be too dependent on drug intake but instead, rely on natural remedies for mild pains and aches.

IF YOU ABSOLUTELY HAVE TO TAKE MEDICATION, TAKE A GOOD DOSE OF PROBIOTICS FOR A WEEK. Most drugs kill both the good and bad bacteria in the digestive system.

AVOID VICES THAT ARE BAD FOR YOUR GUT AND DIGESTIVE HEALTH. They include drinking too much alcohol, caffeine and smoking. They negatively affect the digestive system and cause heartburn and stomach ulcers.

REMOVE GLUTEN AND WHEAT FROM YOUR DIET. Wheat, barley, and rye contain gluten and they all make a leaky gut worse. It raises your body's immune response and causes inflammation. It also allows higher levels of toxins to penetrate through your gut lining.

WHILE YOU ARE STILL RECUPERATING FROM LEAKY GUT, MAKE SURE THAT YOU STAY AWAY FROM EATING LEGUMES AND ALL KINDS OF GRAINS, ESPECIALLY GMO grains with high amounts of lectins, phytates, and other anti-nutrients.

REMOVE ALL REFINED SUGAR FROM YOUR DIET, including the safe sounding types, such as raw sugar and brown sugar. Excessive consumption of refined white sugar causes leaky gut but if you are healing from the condition, other forms of sugar can make it worse. Sugar fuels the growth of the bad bacteria, yeast, and candida in the gut. Refrain from consuming anything loaded with sugar, which includes sauces, ice cream, soft drinks, desserts, and other sweets.

CHAPTER 5

WEIGHT LOSS AND LEAKY GUT SYNDROME

There is correlation between weight loss and gut health. The more of the good microbes you have in your gut, and the more diverse they are, the better chances you have to stay healthy and slim.

Your gut bacteria affect how hungry you are and which foods you crave. As bad bacteria feed on sugar and carbohydrates are sugar, if you suffer from a leaky gut syndrome, you have higher amounts of bad bacteria in your gut, that push you towards binging on carbohydrates: sweets, chocolate, soft drinks, pasta, etc.

The only way to take cravings under control is through the healthy diet. One of the best diets to begin healing your digestive system will be the Gaps Introduction Diet. Start from detoxifying stage and eating home-made bone broth and vegetable soup. Then, gradually start adding supplements (amino-acids, zinc picolinate, Vit B Complex, Vitamin C, calcium, magnesium, vitamin D).

Prolonged fasting, starvation and overeating can significantly alter the composition of gut flora and start a chain of health problems, with the weight gain at the forefront.

An impaired gut causes bloating and can actually stop you from losing weight. When your gut health is compromised, your system will suffer from dysbiosis or having imbalanced bacteria. The condition results in weight gain.

Why it is hard for people with leaky gut to lose weight

There are a number of reasons. Here are the most common ones:

Excessive estrogen.

When your gut is impaired, your liver finds it hard to get rid of your system's excess estrogen. Unlike the popular belief that only women have this kind of hormone, men actually have estrogen as well. Both genders need the hormone for sexual health. Having too much estrogen in the body makes it hard for you to lose weight. This hormone is also pro-growth so too much of it results in increased fat storage.

Chronic inflammation.

A healthy gut lining has lots of tiny pores that drive out the digested food in the stomach to the liver. Digested foods are then processed in the liver before the body can use the energy and nutrients they contain. When the gut is unhealthy, the tendency is for these pores to get clogged, which leads to the irritation of your gut lining. Through time, the pores will get wider, which will result in a leaky gut. The condition allows large food particles and proteins to leak into your bloodstream and cause inflammation all over the body. The condition triggers a boost in the body's production of the stress hormone called cortisol. High cortisol levels are linked to large amounts of belly fat that you will have a hard time getting rid of.

Thyroid problems.

The thyroid gland produces T4 and T3, two hormones needed by the body to properly function. T4 converts into T3, which is needed by the cells to become metabolically active. 20 percent of the conversion process happens in the gut. The conversion will be affected and drastically drop when your gut has more bad than good bacteria. When you have a low thyroid function, it will be harder for you to lose weight, plus, you'll have brittle nails, skin, and hair.

Lipopolysaccharides (LPS) production.

An unhealthy gut becomes home to loads of bad bacteria that excrete waste, a kind of harmful secretion called lipopolysaccharides or LPS. LPS penetrate into the blood and cause inflammation. They also generate the production of new fat cells and increase the size of the existing ones. LPS will make you gain weight and bloated, especially around the belly area.

Effective Methods to Heal Your Digestive System and Lose Weight

There are certain digestive symptoms that happen occasionally, such as diarrhea, constipation, nausea, heartburn, gas, and upset stomach. It becomes a problem when you experience them often to the point wherein the symptoms are already disrupting your daily life.

Here are the natural methods that can help you lose weight:

Add MCT Oil (Medium Chain Triglycerides) to your diet. Studies demonstrate anti-inflammatory and weight-loss benefits of MCTs.

To reduce belly fat, limit carbs in your diet (and eliminate processed and refined carbs completely if possible)

Add soluble and viscous fibers to your diet. They bind water and form a thick gel. The gel slows the movement of food through the digestive system and absorption of nutrients. As a result, you feel full and have lesser appetite. Good sources of soluble fiber include psyllium husk and inulin.

Eat prebiotics and insoluble fiber. Prebiotics feed the good bacteria in the gut and reduce the risk of inflammatory bowel conditions. They promote metabolic health and support the immune system. Good sources of prebiotics include: garlic, leek, asparagus, flaxseeds, nuts, onion, apples. **Insoluble fiber** helps everything in the digestive tract to move along. Good sources of insoluble fiber include: spinach, Brussel sprouts, broccoli, kale.

Consume "real" food. A diet high in refined carbs combined with bad fat intake and lack of exercise, increases your risk of suffering from digestive issues. There are food additives that can worsen gut health and cause inflammation and leaky gut, such as table salt, glucose, and other chemicals. There are artificial sweeteners that cause bloating and other digestive problems. You can prevent all these problems by avoiding food items like these.

Focus on foods rich in nutrients and devoid of toxins and other harmful chemicals.

Drink plenty of filtered and non-chlorinated water. You can add vitamin C powder or raw apple cider vinegar to your water. Add a pinch of Himalayan salt for better absorption of minerals.

Eat food rich in polyphenols. Raw dark chocolate, sulphur-free organic red wine, organic blueberries. <u>Polyphenols</u> enhance the growth of good bacteria and inhibit the growth of bad bacteria.

Eat healthy fats and minimize carbs. Fats aid in nutrient absorption and they make you feel full at a faster rate, making it easier for you to lose weight. Omega-3 fatty acids decrease your chances of suffering from inflammatory bowel conditions. You can get them from sardines, mackerel, salmon, nuts, chia seeds, and flaxseeds.

Practice mindful eating. Eating fast without chewing your food thoroughly causes indigestion, gas, and bloating. You have to pay attention to your food and the process of eating. Eat slowly and focus on the various aspects of what you are eating, such as taste, temperature, and texture. Chewing your food is also a healthy habit because aside from breaking down your food for easy digestion, it prompts the production of saliva necessary to make it easier for the food in the stomach to pass through the intestines.

Learn how to manage your stress. Your digestive system suffers from too much stress. It leads to problems, such as IBS, constipation, diarrhea, and stomach ulcers. Practice relaxation techniques, meditation, yoga, and deep breathing exercises. They will not only manage your stress, but they are also good for your digestion and help in improving your focus and concentration.

Slow down and pause to eliminate overeating. Overeating causes indigestion, bloating, and gas. You can avoid it by listening to your body and paying attention whether you're hungry or full. It takes around 20 minutes for your brain to process that you are already full. To prevent overeating, eat slowly and mindfully. At all times, avoid emotional eating or binging on food when faced with a stressor or whenever you experience strong emotions of happiness of sadness.

Develop a regular exercise routine to improve digestion. Taking a walk after eating a meal helps the food travel to the digestive system at a faster rate. If you are prone to chronic constipation, exercising every day, including a 30-minute walk, will help a lot. Regular physical activity promotes the growth of beneficial gut bacteria such as Bifidobacterium.

Quit the habits that negatively affect your digestion, weight, and overall health:

Too much alcohol causes bleeding in the gastrointestinal tract. It also increases the production of acid in the stomach that results to stomach ulcers, acid reflux, and heartburn.

Smoking causes digestive problems and doubles your risk of acid reflux.

Stop late-night eating. When you lie down while your stomach is still full, the tendency is for the food you ate to rise up, which will lead to heartburn and increased risk of reflux symptoms. You have to give enough time for your body to digest food and move it from the stomach to the small intestine before you sleep. It is recommended to give an allowance of at least four hours from your last meal to your sleeping time.

Don't ignore the urge to go to the loo. Delaying it, causes in constipation, bloating, and may end up in more serious digestive issues.

Stop drinking with meals. It dilutes stomach acid and digestive enzymes, making it harder for your body to digest food properly. It is best to drink minimum 30mins before the meal or 2 hours after.

CHAPTER 6

THE 10 BEST NATURAL WAYS TO
SUPPORT THE IMMUNE SYSTEM

T aking care of the immune system doesn't need to be expensive. Instead of getting yourself treated and taking medications with hefty price tags, first try implementing natural ways to make your immune system stronger.

Here are the top 10 ways to get this done:

As the first line of defense, adapt to a healthy lifestyle. You may have been told about this over and over again but there's a good reason behind it. A healthy lifestyle doesn't only protect your gut or help you lose weight, it keeps your immune system and overall health in top shape.

Along with a healthy diet, supplement with multivitamins needed by your immune system. Vitamin A, B, C, D, and E. Vitamins B2 and B6 to help you in avoiding illnesses and boosting your immune response.

Use turmeric in your foods. This popular spice can be added to dishes and there are also turmeric products that you can drink. It makes the immune system stronger and helps in preventing illnesses. It has also potent anti-inflammatory properties. Turmeric extracts have been proven effective in easing arthritis pain, slowing down the progress of Alzheimer's and in preventing cancer.

Pamper yourself with a long relaxing bath with Epsom salt or essential oils. No matter how busy you are, never forget to take good care of yourself. If you are often sleep deprived, pause and take a breather once in a while or at the end of each week. Pampering yourself doesn't have to be lavish. A nice hot bath with aromatherapy scents or Epsom salt will help in relieving your stress and make it easier for you to get quality sleep at a longer time. Your body will be able to repair and recharge itself by having a good sleep and feeling relaxed. Your immune system will suffer if you will allow yourself to wallow on problems and stress without taking the time to recharge and get rid of the negative vibes.

Avoid taking over-the-counter medications and other drugs as much as possible. It takes 3 to 6 months for your microbiome to recover from taking antibiotic treatment for one week. Always take them with caution and do not take antibiotics when you are not even certain that you have a bacterial infection. You must also limit your intake of nonsteroidal anti-inflammatories, ibuprofen, and other painkillers because they have a negative effect on your immune and gut health.

Try herbal remedies for relief and to boost your immune system. If you are under any kinds of medications, talk to your doctor first about your intentions to try herbal medications.

Here are some of the herbs effective in healing and in making the immune system stronger:

Oregano. In Greek, it means "joy of the mountain." This herb contains volatile oils needed for a healthy immune system and microbiome. It's a good source of natural antioxidants and supports healthy digestive flora. It has phytochemicals that aid the natural resistance of the body, plus it is also used in cooking in different countries, especially in Europe.

Echinacea. This herb is also called the purple coneflower and is among the most researched herbs in the world. According to studies, different parts of the different species of this herb offer various benefits, reason why they are often used together. This herb boosts the immune system and supports its healthy response.

Black Elderberry. Its deep purple color is due to its natural concentration of anthocyanins that act as antioxidants and support healthy immune response. Its tree is often referred to as the tree of music because Native Americans used to make flutes from its branches. You can consume it in various ways, such as snacking on the berries or use as flavoring to wine, syrups or jams.

Olive Leaf. It contains oleurpein and antioxidant properties that support the immune system and cardiovascular health.

Astragalus. This herb has been used in Chinese medicine since ancient times. It supports the immune system at the cellular level and gives you resistance against sicknesses and stressors. It is considered an adaptogen since it supports your adrenals, which makes it easier for you to cope with daily stresses,

Consume colostrum.

It is the first milk that comes from nursing mammals loaded with lactoferrin and other anti-inflammatory substances and protective antibodies. This is the reason why many people promote breastfeeding for babies. The effects of colostrum in babies will support them during their first years while their immune system is still getting developed. Even adults nowadays can consume and benefit from colostrum.

You can now get it in powder form, obtained from grass-fed goats, cows, and other mammals. You can mix it in juice, water, or smoothies.

Try healing mushroom that act like turbo-shots for your immune system:

Shiitake. You can find this in many grocery stores. It's delicious and can be used in a variety of dishes. It is rich in beta glucans that make your white blood cells stronger and responsible in strengthening your immune system.

Maitake. This mushroom variety is also delicious, plus it fights off bad bacteria in the body by increasing your immune cells.

Reishi. It is loaded with anti-cancer and antiviral properties. This mushroom variety is not edible but you can consume it as a tea or tincture or take as a dried capsule.

Turkey Tail. It increases Bifidobacterium spp. And Lactobacillus spp. – two key species of bacteria that inoculate our gut, stabilize it and act as a prebiotic to modulate a diverse microbiome after the course of antibiotics.

Lion's Mane. It is gastroprotective, decreasing inflammatory and immune responses

Chaga. It is called the mother of all the antioxidants. It calms down the immune system, lowers the blood pressure and blood sugar.

Use antimicrobials to prevent and heal infections.

For starters, here are some food items that you can incorporate in your meals for delicious dishes that help in boosting your immunity and overall health:

Oregano oil. You can take it internally to fight off yeast infections. It can also be applied topically to help in healing MRSA or antibiotic-resistant staph infections of the skin. The oil contains antifungal, antiviral, and antimicrobial properties.

Raw garlic. It contains allicin, a potent sulfur compound effective in treating SIBO or small-intestinal bacterial overgrowth and GI infections and in getting rid of yeast infections and parasites. You can take one piece of raw garlic when you see early signs of an infection or you can also use allicin extract in concentrated form.

Manuka honey. This is native to Australia and New Zealand, where it is registered as a product for wound-care. It can be ingested to boost the effects of antibiotics or applied topically to ward off bacteria. It is known for its antimicrobial, anti-inflammatory, and immune-boosting properties.

Clove oil. It is anti-inflammatory and antimicrobial. It reduces the bacteria that cause gum disease and creates a balanced oral microbiome.

Other anti-fungal essential oils:

Lemongrass essential oil,

Lavender essential oil,

Tea Tree Essential Oil,

Thyme Essential Oil,

Cinnamon Bark Essential Oil.

Get a good massage every once in a while.

It is a good therapy for aching muscles and joints. It also alleviates pain, stiffness and arthritis. It boosts the body's production of serotonin that fights off stress. It also increases the activity of the body's white blood cells, which help your system in warding off bacteria and germs.

CHAPTER 7

EASY AND DELICIOUS GUT FRIENDLY RECIPES

O ne of the ways to heal a leaky gut is through the food you eat. Just because you are on your way to heal your gut, it does not mean you have to eat boring food. Below are some of the most delicious and nutritious recipes that are gut-friendly, inexpensive and simple to make.

With the recipes that use beef as an ingredient, use organic grass-fed beef. Most of the ingredients used here are gut-friendly and are not likely to let you develop any adverse food reactions.

All the recipes are based on the GAPS Diet approach. They are mostly low carb, gluten free, grain free, and soy free. No vegetable oils were used for frying and every ingredient is accessible – relatively inexpensive and can be found in your local stores.

ANTI-INFLAMMATORY GUT-FRIENDLY BREAKFASTS

Chia Seed-Coconut Yogurt Smoothie Bowl

While this recipe is dairy-free, it has a creamy texture and a burst of flavor. The addition of chia seeds guarantees extra nutrients, and blueberries add color and a burst of antioxidants.

Preparation Time: 5 Minutes

Makes 2 to 3 Servings

Ingredients:

- 2 dates, halved and pitted (you can skip this if you don't want it too sweet)
- 3 organic bananas (ripe, sliced)
- ¼ cup unsweetened coconut water
- 2 cups coconut milk yogurt (can be plain yogurt or any yogurt of your choice)
- ¼ cup chia seeds
- 1 small container organic blueberries
- 1/3 cup roasted flaked almonds
- Toppings: sliced strawberries, hemp seeds, raspberries, blackberries (to give yourself greater energy boost, try maca powder, raw cacao or cinnamon)

In a food processor, put in the bananas, dates, yogurt, coconut water, and blueberries. Blend until you get a smooth consistency. Add chia seeds and leave for 5 minutes to allow chia to swell.

Place in bowls and top with sliced strawberries, hemp seeds, raspberries, blackberries, maca, cacao, cinnamon. Scatter roasted almond flakes.

Flourless Banana Pancakes

These flour-less, gluten-free pancakes are easy to make and delicious. You only need a few ingredients, and you can prepare them in no time.

Preparation Time: 15 Minutes

Makes 1 Serving

Ingredients:

- 3 organic free-range eggs
- 1 banana (ripe), mashed
- 1 teaspoon vanilla extract
- 1 teaspoon cinnamon
- Ghee
- Himalayan salt, to taste

Place all ingredients in a bowl. Mix well. In a pan with melted ghee, pour the batter. Cook over medium heat until small bubbles form on top. Flip the pancakes, and cook further. Serve hot.

Warming Sweet Potato Porridge Bowl

The recipe has loads of coconut with natural antimicrobial properties and lauric acid. It is also rich in prebiotics, which feed the good bacteria in the gut.

Yield: 2 servings

Ingredients:

- 1/2 cup unsweetened coconut flakes (or roasted flaked almonds)
- 1/2 cup pomegranate seeds
- A pinch of salt
- 1/8 teaspoon ground cinnamon
- 1 tsp pure vanilla extract
- 1/4 cup coconut butter
- 1 1/2 cups full-fat coconut milk
- 2 cups cooked sweet potato

Method:

Put the cooked sweet potato, vanilla, cinnamon, salt, coconut milk, and coconut butter in a food processor. Process until smooth. Transfer to a saucepan over low flame. Cook for 10 minutes while stirring often. Gradually add coconut milk as you stir until you've reached your desired consistency.

Garnish with coconut flakes (flaked almonds) and pomegranate seeds. Serve warm for maximum benefits.

Blueberry and Almond Oatmeal Muffins

This super healthy variation of breakfast muffins is packed with nutritious ingredients, gluten free, dairy free, refined sugar free and made with mix of almond and oat flour. Simply incredible.

Preparation Time: 10 Minutes

Makes 9 Muffins

Ingredients:

- 1 cup gluten free oat flour (plus 2 spoons)

- 1 cup almond flour

- 2 eggs (room temperature, beaten)

- ½ cup unsweetened almond milk (or any dairy free milk you like)

- 1 tablespoon olive oil

- 1 cup fresh organic blueberries

- 1 teaspoon apple cider vinegar (can be lemon juice)

- 1 teaspoon vanilla extract

- Almond essence (3-4 drops)

- ½ cup flaked almonds

- 1/3 cup Xylitol sweetener (can be maple syrup if you don't mind carbs)

- ¾ teaspoon baking soda

- ¼ teaspoon Himalayan/Sea salt

Method:

Preheat the oven to 350°F. Line 9 muffin cups with liners and spray the inside of the liners with the nonstick cooking spray.

In a large bowl combine oat flour, almond flour, salt and baking soda (two extra tablespoons of flour reserve for later).

In a separate bowl beat eggs, Xylitol (maple syrop), almond milk, almond essence, vanilla extract, olive oil and apple cider vinegar. Mix until well combined and smooth.

Add dry ingredients to wet ingredients and stir with spatula.

In a small bowl toss blueberries and oat flour together and gently fold into the batter.

Divide batter evenly between muffin cups, filling ¾ of the way full. Scatter the flaked almonds on top. Bake for 18-25 minutes or until well risen, springy to the touch and golden brown.

Transfer pan with muffins to a wire rack and cool for 10 minutes then remove muffins form a wire rack and leave to cool completely.

Recipe notes:

- You can use raspberries instead of blueberries and the muffins will taste equally amazing.

- To make this recipe vegan, use flaxseed meal instead of eggs. Here's how to do it:

2 tablespoons flaxseed meal mix with 6 tablespoons lukewarm water. Allow to sit for 5 minutes before using in this recipe.

Sweet Potato Hash

If you want a spin to your breakfast potato hash, use sweet potato instead of regular potato. Why sweet potatoes? They are high in fiber, vitamin A, B3, B5, B6, C, magnesium and copper. They have a relatively low glycemic index, and they are anti-inflammatory food.

Preparation Time: 40 Minutes

Makes 3 to 4 Servings

Ingredients:

- 2 cubed organic sweet potatoes
- 1 red onion (medium), chopped
- 2 tablespoons avocado oil
- 2 cloves organic garlic, minced
- 1 chopped red bell pepper
- ½ teaspoon oregano
- ½ teaspoon powdered garlic
- ½ teaspoon paprika

Toppings:

- Fresh cilantro

- 1 organic free range egg

- Hot pepper sauce (sugar free)

Preheat the oven to 350°F. Use parchment paper to line a baking sheet. Place all the ingredients (except the toppings) on the sheet, and hand-toss the oil until it coats the sweet potato cubes.

Bake until potatoes become tender or for about 30 minutes, and are easily pierced by a fork. Set on a plate. Top with egg (cooked in your preferred way), hot sauce, and cilantro.

Carrot and Sausage Hash

Organic sausage contains healthy fat that helps in stabilizing blood sugar enough to maintain your energy levels. You'll get a rich amount of prebiotic fibers from carrots that the good bacteria in the gut can feed on. The recipe also contains natural anti-microbial sources, such as scallions and coconut oil.

Yield: 4 servings

Ingredients:

- 2 scallions

- 1 teaspoon onion powder

- 1 teaspoon Himalayan salt

- 5 cups grated organic carrots

- 2 tablespoons coconut oil
- 1pound organic lose ground pork sausage

Method:

Put scallions, onion powder, salt, and grated carrots in a bowl. Toss until combined.

Heat oil in a pan over medium flame. Add sausage and break it into smaller pieces using a wooden spoon as you cook. Stir until soft. Transfer the cooked sausage to a plate but leave the grease in the pan.

Add the carrot mixture to the same pan where you cooked the sausage. Cook until tender while stirring often. Turn off the heat and put the sausage back to the pan. Mix until combined.

Serve while warm.

Bacon and Turnip Hash

The neutral flavor and slight starchiness of turnips make them a great alternative to potato for your breakfast meals. Bacon contains antimicrobial saturated fat that keeps your gut happy. This recipe also has garlic and onion, both loaded with sulfur, which speeds up the detoxification process and zucchini that contains fiber and minerals.

Yield: 4 servings

Ingredients:

- 1/8 teaspoon garlic powder

- 1/2 cup chopped red onion

- 1 small zucchini (grated)

- Himalayan salt and pepper to taste

- 2 large turnips (grated)

- 1pound pasture-raised or organic bacon (chopped)

Method:

Cook bacon in a preheated skillet over medium-high flame until crispy. Transfer to a plate and leave about 3 tablespoons of the grease in the skillet. Strain the rest of the oil and reserve for future use.

Put zucchini and turnips in a strainer. Firmly press using your hands to force out excess liquids.

Place skillet with the bacon grease over medium flame. Add onion and stir until cooked. Stir in the veggies and stir until all the pieces are coated with grease. Leave to cook for about 15 minutes or until crispy while occasionally stirring. Season with garlic powder, salt, and pepper. Add the cooked bacon and stir until combined.

Wild Cod with Asparagus Breakfast Delight

Wild Cod is loaded with omega-3s, choline, iodine, and selenium. This recipe also has ingredients rich in sulfur for detox, such as scallions, spinach, garlic, and asparagus. It also requires ginger, which contains antimicrobial oils that get rid of bacteria and yeast.

Yield: 4 servings

Ingredients:

- 1 tablespoon virgin olive oil or coconut oil
- 2 tablespoons coconut aminos
- 1 tablespoon grated fresh ginger
- 2 garlic cloves (minced)
- Salt and pepper to taste
- 2 scallions (thinly sliced)
- 8 cups fresh spinach
- 1 bunch asparagus (ends trimmed and sliced)
- 4 wild cod fillets

Method:

Divide parchment paper into 4 with an approximate length of 12 inches. Put 2 cups of spinach on each piece of parchment paper. Top each pile with a fish, scallion, and asparagus.

Put ginger, garlic, sesame oil, coconut aminos, salt, and pepper in a bowl. Whisk until combined. Divide sauce into 4 and pour on top of each pile.

Fold each parchment paper into small packets and wrap the ends tightly.

Bake in a preheated oven at 425 degrees for 15 minutes. Transfer to a plate and serve.

Eggs and Baked Artichokes Hash

Yield: 3 servings

Ingredients:

- 3 teaspoons coconut oil or ghee

- Salt and freshly ground pepper to taste

- 2 tablespoons chopped fresh parsley

- 1 tablespoon capers

- Ground or freshly grated turmeric to taste

- 6 organic eggs

- 1 pound Jerusalem artichokes (peeled and sliced)

- 1/2 cup vegetable broth

Method:

Heat oil in a pan over medium flame. Add the artichokes, parsley, and capers. Cook for 3 minutes while stirring often. Pour in the broth and leave to simmer for 3 minutes. Season with turmeric, salt, and pepper. Transfer to a casserole baking dish and top with eggs.

Bake dish in a preheated oven at 400 degrees for 10 minutes. Transfer to a wire rack to cool.

Slice and serve.

Probiotic Rich Sauerkraut with Eggs

Yield: 2 servings

Ingredients:

- 4 large organic eggs
- 1 cup organic sauerkraut
- 2 tablespoons ghee or coconut oil
- 1/2 teaspoon Himalayan salt
- 1 small red onion (diced)
- 1 garlic clove (minced)

Method:

Whisk eggs in a bowl. Add water and salt and continue whisking until foamy. Set aside.

Heat oil in a pan over medium-high flame. Add onion and sauté for 1 minute. Add garlic and cook for another minute. Add the egg mixture, scramble, and cook until you get your preferred consistency. Transfer to a plate, top with sauerkraut, and serve.

Scotch Eggs

Yield: 6 servings

Ingredients:

- 1 1/2 teaspoons celery salt

- 1/2 teaspoon garlic powder

- 1/2 teaspoon smoked paprika

- 1/2 teaspoon dried thyme

- 1/4 teaspoon celery seed

- 6 large organic eggs

- 1 1/2 pounds organic ground pork

- 5 cups water

- 3 tablespoons sea salt

- 2 tablespoons ghee or coconut oil

- 3 cups homemade ketchup

- 3 cups arugula

Method:

Put water and salt in a pot over high flame. Bring to a boil. Reduce heat to medium-low. Add eggs, cover the pot, and continue boiling for 10 minutes.

In a bowl, put celery salt, garlic powder, smoked paprika, dried thyme, and celery seed. Mix well. Add meat and use your hands to combine everything. Divide mixture into 6 and form them into meatballs. Set aside.

Put the cooked eggs in a bowl filled with ice water and peel.

Press each meatball until flat and put an egg inside. Wrap egg with the meatball. Repeat the process with the rest of the meatballs and eggs.

Heat oil in a pan over medium flame. Put all the meat-covered eggs until all sides are browned. Transfer to a baking dish. Bake in a preheated oven at 400 degrees for 10 minutes. Allow to cool and slice.

Arrange arugula in a plate. Place the sliced Scotch eggs on top and drizzle with homemade ketchup.

Spicy Deviled Eggs

Yield: 3 servings

Ingredients:

- 2 tablespoons full fat Greek yogurt
- 6 hard-boiled eggs (peeled)
- 1/2 teaspoon dill
- 1/8 teaspoon salt
- 1/4 teaspoon spicy mustard
- A dash of paprika and black pepper

Method:

Slice each egg in half. Scoop out the egg yolks and place 3 yolks in a bowl. Reserve the rest for future use. Set aside the white part.

Add yogurt to the yolks. Mash until combined. Gradually add dill, mustard, and salt as you mash.

Place a scoop of the mixture into each half of the egg white. Sprinkle with paprika and pepper.

DELICIOUS PROTEIN-RICH AND VITAMIN-PACKED LUNCHES

Beef Sukiyaki

Yield: 6 servings

Ingredients:

- 2 tablespoons rice wine vinegar
- 2 cups of onion (thinly sliced)
- 2 cups of celery (cut into strips)
- 1 1/2 pounds organic flank steak (thinly sliced)
- 5 green onions (cut diagonally)
- 3 garlic cloves (minced)
- 1/2 cup tamari
- 4 cups bok choy
- 1 tablespoon olive oil
- 2 tablespoons beef stock
- 2 cups cabbage (shredded)
- 2 cups mushrooms (sliced)

Method:

Prepare the marinade. In a bowl, put the tamari, vinegar, 2 tablespoons of stock, and garlic. Mix until combined. Add the meat and leave to soak for at least 4 hours.

Chop and prepare the vegetables.

Transfer the marinated meat to a plate.

Add 1 3/4 cups of stock to the marinade. Set aside.

Heat a tablespoon of water and oil in a pan over medium flame. Cook the meat for 2 minutes and transfer the meat to a plate.

Cook the onion and celery in the pan. Add 1/4 cup of the marinade, cabbage, and bok choy. Cover the pan and leave to cook for 2 minutes. Reduce heat to low. Add the rest of the marinade, mushrooms, green onions, and cooked meat. Stir until combined.

Beef with Mushroom, Egg, and Spinach

Yield: 1 serving

Ingredients:

- 1/2 cup mushrooms (chopped)
- 1 hard-boiled egg (peeled and sliced)
- 2 cups fresh spinach (chopped)
- 1/2 tablespoon olive oil
- 1/2 tablespoon basil
- Tamari to taste
- 1 garlic clove (minced)

- 1/4 pound of extra lean ground beef

Method:

Heat oil in a skillet over medium flame. Add garlic and cook for a couple of minutes. Add meat and cook until both sides are browned. Put the mushrooms, spinach, basil, and tamari. Turn heat to low and leave to cook until the spinach has wilted. Transfer to a plate.

Arrange sliced eggs on top of the dish. Serve while warm.

Chicken Nuggets

You'll be using dark meat chicken for this recipe, which has gut and immune boosting fatty acids, plus vitamins A and D. Coconut or cassava flour, which you will use to coat the meat is rich in prebiotic fibers. The recipe also calls for spices with antimicrobial properties.

Yield: 4 servings

Ingredients:

- 1/4 cup coconut flour or cassava flour
- 1/2 teaspoon salt
- 1 teaspoon onion powder
- 1 teaspoon garlic powder
- 1/4 cup coconut oil (for frying)
- 1 teaspoon dried oregano
- 1 pound boneless and skinless chicken thighs (sliced into

1-inch thickness)

Method:

In a bowl, mix to combine salt, spices, and flour. Add the sliced meat and toss until evenly coated.

Heat oil in a pan. Place half of the coated chicken and cook until both sides are browned. Transfer to a plate lined with paper towels. Cook the rest of the chicken nuggets.

Serve nuggets with a side salad or mustard for dipping.

Salmon with Cauliflower Steak

The recipe calls for salmon and avocado, both loaded with healthy fats and cauliflower with prebiotics and vitamin C. It also has radishes that work in stimulating the digestive juices that fight off bad gut bacteria and break down food.

Yield: 4 to 6 servings

Ingredients:

- 4 radishes (thinly sliced)
- 1 avocado (diced)
- 1/2 cup cilantro (chopped)
- 1 teaspoon salt
- 2 tablespoons garlic powder
- 1 teaspoon oregano

- 2 tablespoons ground cumin

- 1 lime, zest and juice

- 1/4 cup olive oil or avocado oil

- 2 large heads cauliflower (leaves removed)

- 1 pound wild-caught salmon

Method:

Rinse cauliflower and slice into steaks with 3-inch thickness.

Whisk lime juice and olive oil in a bowl.

In another bowl, mix to combine salt and all the dry spices.

Arrange the cauliflower steaks in a tray. Brush all sides with olive oil and lime and sprinkle with the spice mixture.

Grill the cauliflower steaks. Baste with the oil mixture as you cook and sprinkle with the spice mixture.

Grill salmon until both sides are done. Cover the grill and leave for 5 minutes. Flip the salmon and cauliflower, cover the grill, and continue cooking for 5 minutes.

Prepare the dipping. Put the diced avocado, chopped cilantro, and sliced radishes in a bowl. Mix until combined. Season with salt.

Place salmon on a platter. Add the cauliflower steak on the side and top with the dipping.

Bison with Veggies

It is essential to eat high-quality red meat, such as grass-fed bison and beef, in moderation. They are rich in vitamin B6, selenium, niacin, zinc, and iron. Zinc is essential to gut health and it boosts the immune system. Selenium fights against free-radical damage and iron aids in carrying oxygen from the lungs to the different tissues in the body.

Yield: 4 servings

Ingredients:

- 10 button or baby Bella mushrooms (thinly sliced)
- 1 small zucchini (thinly sliced)
- 2 tablespoon kalamata olive tapenade
- 1 small white onion (thinly sliced)
- 1 teaspoon sea salt
- 1 tablespoon dried basil
- 1 tablespoon onion powder
- 1 tablespoon garlic powder
- 3 tablespoons coconut flour
- 1 pound ground bison

Method:

Put salt, spices, and flour in a bowl. Mix until combined. Add the bison. Mix using your hands until all sides of the meat are coated.

Transfer to a glass baking dish and firmly press as thinly as you can. Spread top with a thin layer of the Kalamata olive spread. Top with mushrooms, zucchini, and onion.

Bake in a preheated oven at 400 degrees for 25 minutes.

Turkey Meatball Wraps

This recipe calls for dark meat turkey, which is loaded with healthy fats and selenium. Selenium helps in sealing a leaky gut while healthy fats control blood sugar. It also contains magnesium and potassium sources, such as lettuce and cucumber, and antibacterial spices, namely coriander, cumin, cilantro, parsley, and garlic.

Yield: 5 servings

Ingredients:

- 20 lettuce leaves (Bibb or Boston)
- 1/2 teaspoon ground coriander
- 1/2 teaspoon ground cumin
- Cucumber slices (optional for garnish)
- Salt to taste
- 1/4 cup cilantro (chopped)
- 1/4 cup parsley (chopped0
- 1 garlic clove (minced)
- 1/2 cup red onion (diced)

- 1 pound ground dark meat turkey

Method:

Put meat in a bowl. Add cumin, salt, coriander, parsley, garlic, and onion. Mix well. Use your hands to form small meatballs from the mixture. Arrange them on a baking sheet lined with parchment paper. Bake in a preheated oven at 425 degrees for 20 minutes.

Arrange lettuce leaves on a plate. Put the meatballs on top and garnish with the cucumber slices.

Healthy Turkey Wrap

It is as tasty as a turkey club but doesn't contain inflammatory ingredients. The meat of turkey is generally good for gut health since it is a rich source of selenium. The recipe contains sulfur and magnesium from lettuce and sprouts, beta-carotene from carrots, and monounsaturated fats from avocado.

Yield: 2 servings

Ingredients:

- 1/2 cup alfalfa sprouts
- 4 romaine lettuce leaves
- 2 tablespoons organic mustard
- 1/2 cup shredded carrots
- 8 slices organic turkey lunch meat (thinly sliced)
- 1 avocado (mashed)

- 2 grain-free and gluten-free tortillas

Method:

Place tortillas in a dry pan over low heat and leave to warm until pliable. Transfer to a plate.

Divide half of the mashed avocado into the 2 tortillas and spread all over. Add mustard and spread on top of the avocado. Arrange turkey slices, lettuce, sprouts, and shredded carrots on top. Fold each tortilla and serve.

Coconut Curry Meatballs

Yield: 24 meatballs

Ingredients:

- 1 egg
- 1/2 cup shredded coconut
- A handful of parsley
- 2 garlic cloves
- 1 carrot (grated)
- 650 grams chicken (boneless and skinless)
- 1/2 teaspoon salt
- 2 teaspoons curry powder

Method:

Whisk the egg in a bowl. Chop the rest of the ingredients before adding to the bowl. Mix well. Use your hands to form 24 meatballs from the mixture.

Heat oil in a pan over medium-high flame. Cook the meatballs in batches until browned. Transfer to a platter lined with paper towels to drain excess oil.

Serve at once.

Zucchini Noodles with Beef and Broccoli

Beef is loaded with iron and zinc, broccoli is rich in sulfur, and zucchini is a good source of magnesium. The recipe also contains antifungal and antibacterial spices.

Yield: 4 servings

Ingredients:

- 12 ounces zucchini noodles (or kelp noodles)
- 1/4 teaspoon black pepper
- 1/4 teaspoon salt
- 1/2 cup basil (minced)
- 1/4 cup olive tapenade (for garnish)
- 12 ounces boneless beef sirloin steak (thinly sliced)
- 1/4 cup olive oil
- 1 cup bone broth
- 5 garlic cloves (minced)
- 1 teaspoon dried oregano
- 1 medium sweet onion (thinly sliced)
- 3 cups broccoli florets (fresh or frozen)

Method:

Heat 2 tablespoons of olive oil in a skillet over medium flame. Add onion and garlic and cook for 5 minutes while frequently stirring.

Transfer to a small bowl and set aside.

Put the steak strips in the same skillet where you cooked garlic and onion. Season with salt, pepper, and oregano. Cook for 5 minutes. Transfer to a plate and set aside.

Put the rest of the oil in the skillet. Once heated, add the bone broth and broccoli. Cook for about 4 minutes. Put back the garlic, onion, and meat to the skillet. Add basil and stir. Leave to cook for a couple of minutes.

To serve, place a portion of the noodles on a plate. Add broccoli and beef mixture on top and a dollop of olive tapenade to garnish.

Sweet Potatoes with Bacon

Yield: 2 servings

Ingredients:

- 1 avocado (cubed)

- 1 scallion (chopped)

- 4 bacon slices

- 2 medium sweet potatoes (pre-cooked)

- 3 garlic cloves (sliced)

- 1 tablespoon coconut oil

- 2 cups fresh spinach

- 1 large sweet onion (sliced)

Method:

Cook bacon slice in a skillet over medium flame until crispy. Transfer to a plate but leave bacon grease in the skillet. Set aside.

Add a tablespoon of coconut oil in the skillet. Put the garlic and onion and cook for 30 minutes while stirring often. Transfer to a bowl and set aside.

Put the spinach in the skillet until tender.

Slice the precooked potatoes in half. Top each half with the cooked ingredients and avocado.

Serve while warm.

Yummy Flank Steak

Yield: 4 servings

Ingredients:

- 2 tablespoons tamari
- 1 pound flank steak (trim the fat)
- 2 garlic cloves (crushed)
- 1 tablespoon ginger root (peeled and diced)
- 1/4 cup olive oil

Method:

Put oil, garlic, tamari, and ginger in a Ziploc bag. Seal the bag and shake until combined. Put the meat inside the bag, seal, and shake.

Refrigerate for 8 hours to marinate, turning the bag over every 2 hours.

Grease a broiler pan and place the marinated meat in it. Pour the marinade in a bowl for basting.

Cook the meat until both sides are cooked. Baste it as often as needed.

Slice and serve.

Stir-Fried Shrimp and Baby Bok Choy

Shrimp contains minerals, such as B vitamin choline, iodine, and selenium and loaded with fatty acids. The recipe also calls for ginger with antibacterial properties, bok choy with magnesium and sulfur, and mushrooms that contain selenium.

Yield: 4 servings

Ingredients:

- 1 pound shrimp (peeled and deveined)
- 1 teaspoon sesame oil
- 1 tablespoon coconut aminos
- Salt and white pepper to taste
- 1 teaspoon tapioca starch
- 1/2 cup bone broth
- 1/2 teaspoon fresh ginger (minced)

- 1 pound baby Bella mushrooms (stems removed, slice the caps)

- 2 garlic cloves (minced)

- 8 baby bok choy (stems removed, chopped into 1-inch pieces)

Method:

In a bowl, put the coconut aminos, white pepper, tapioca starch, and starch.

Heat oil in a skillet over medium-high flame. Add mushrooms and bok choy and cook while occasionally stirring. Stir in garlic and ginger and cook for a couple of minutes. Add the veggies and shrimp and cook for 3 minutes. Create a hole in the middle of the skillet. Add the starch and broth mixture and leave to simmer for 2 minutes. Mix well until combined.

You can serve the dish along with cauliflower rice.

Grilled Turkey with Lemon Mustard

Yield: 2 servings

Ingredients:

- 2 tablespoons mustard

- 2 tablespoons fresh parsley (chopped)

- 1 pound turkey breast cutlets

- Spike, paprika, and black pepper to taste

- 1 teaspoon fresh lemon juice
- 1 tablespoon mayonnaise

Method:

1. Rinse the turkey breast cutlets and use paper towels to pat them dry. Arrange them on a greased broiler pan.

2. In a bowl, mix to combine spike, mayonnaise, mustard, and lemon juice. Brush the meat with the mixture.

3. Broil meat for 5 minutes. Turn them over, baste, and sprinkle with pepper and paprika. Broil for 1 more minute.

4. Top with chopped parsley before serving.

Baked Salmon in Teriyaki Sauce

You can easily clean up this easy-to-make baked salmon dish. Baking the salmon in foil keeps the flavors locked and the fish moist. It has also packed with omega-3 fatty acids for a heart-healthy treat.

Preparation Time: 30 Minutes

Makes 4 Servings

Ingredients:

- 2 tablespoons coconut sugar
- 1/3 cup coconut aminos
- 3 tablespoons lemon juice
- ¼ cup virgin olive oil

- 1 teaspoon ground garlic

- 3 garlic cloves, minced

- 4 salmon fillets (6 ounces each) with skin on, wild-caught

- Black pepper and Himalayan salt for seasoning

- Coconut oil for brushing

Method:

Use foil to line a baking sheet. Preheat the oven to 375°F. In a small bowl, whisk together the coconut sugar, coconut aminos, lemon juice, sesame oil, mustard, garlic, pepper and sea salt.

Put salmon on the prepared sheet and fold up the foil's four sides. Spoon the whisked mixture over the fish. Fold the foil's sides over the salmon, completely covering and closing the packet.

Bake in the oven for about 15 to 20 minutes or until the salmon is cooked through.

Beef Stew

This healthy beef stew is also good for the gut, and it is full of protein and vegetables. Prepare this stew to enjoy on a cold day.

Preparation Time: 8 to 10 Hours

Makes 3 to 6 Servings

Ingredients:

- 1 to 2 pounds beef chuck
- 2 peeled onions, chopped
- Black pepper and Himalayan salt to taste
- 6 garlic cloves
- 6 sprigs thyme, chopped
- 6 sprigs parsley, chopped
- 6 cups bone broth, beef
- Chopped carrots
- Peeled rutabaga, chopped
- Chopped celery
- 2 to 4 tablespoons coconut aminos

Method:

Place all the ingredients in a crock-pot or slow cooker. Cook on low for 8 to 10 hours. Serve hot.

Chicken Enchilada

An enchilada is a type of tortilla filled with various ingredients and topped with a sauce. Unfortunately, while enchiladas are delicious, they are not always healthy especially if they have toppings like rich creamy sauces.

Instead of rich cheese, this enchilada recipe uses raw cheese. They are also baked and the wraps used (coconut, not corn) are gluten-free.

Preparation Time: 10 Minutes

Total Preparation Time (including baking): 30 Minutes

Makes 7 to 8 Servings

Ingredients:

- 1 pound cooked chicken tenders, chopped
- 7 to 8 coconut wraps
- 1 chopped red onion
- 1 chopped yellow squash
- 1 ½ cups salsa verde
- 1 package (4 ounces) goat cheese
- Shredded raw cheese
- Chopped cilantro
- Chopped green onions

Method:

Heat the oven to 350°F. On each wrap, arrange the chicken, onion, goat cheese, and squash. Roll. Put the rolls in an 8"x10" baking dish. Once you have placed the rolls, top with raw cheese and salsa verde.

Bake for 15 to 20 minutes. Serve and top with green onions and cilantro.

Lamb Roast with Garlic & Rosemary

This is an easy roast recipe to make, and you can leave it overnight and enjoy it during the next day's lunch or dinner. It is easy to make, healthy, and everyone in the family would love it. Choose organic lamb to make the roast dish gut-friendly.

Preparation Time: 6 to 10 Hours

Makes 2 to 4 Servings

Ingredients:

- 1 leg of organic lamb to fit crock pot
- Water to cover the leg of lamb
- 2 tablespoons coconut vinegar (or apple cider vinegar)
- 2 tablespoons organic Worcester sauce
- 1 teaspoon Himalayan salt
- 6 cloves garlic
- 1 teaspoon rosemary
- 1 teaspoon black pepper
- Chopped butternut squash, onions, and carrots

Method:

Put all the ingredients in a slow cooker or crock-pot. Depending on lamb size and settings, cook on low for 6 to 10 hours.

Crispy Salmon Stir Fry

This dieter's favorite is full of protein, omega 3 fatty acids, and vegetables. You can whip up this recipe for lunch or dinner in no time.

Preparation Time: 20 Minutes

Makes 2 to 4 Servings

Ingredients:

- 1 tablespoon coconut oil
- ¼ cup coconut aminos
- 2 teaspoon virgin olive oil
- 2 teaspoons brown rice vinegar
- 4 cloves garlic, minced
- 1 cup peppers, chopped
- 1 cup onion, chopped
- 1 pound Alaskan salmon (wild-caught), skinned and sliced into 1 ½-inch cubes
- 1 ½ cups mushrooms, chopped
- 2 cups broccoli florets, chopped
- 1 tablespoon sesame seeds
- 1 tablespoon ginger (fresh), finely chopped

Method:

Over medium heat, add coconut oil, coconut aminos, sesame oil, and vinegar in a large skillet. Add the onions, peppers, and garlic. Cook until the onions become translucent. Add the salmon. Add the ginger, mushrooms, and broccoli. Cook until the salmon reaches an internal temperature of 145°F. Use sesame seeds as toppings to the salmon mixture. Serve hot.

Turkey Meatballs with Herbs

This delicious meatball soup is great for a winter day. It is also nutritious as it has lots of lean protein and healthy vegetables, and it is good for the gut.

Preparation Time: 60 Minutes

Makes 2 to 4 Servings

Ingredients:

- 1 pound turkey, ground
- ¼ cup minced onion
- 2 eggs
- ½ teaspoon onion powder
- 1 teaspoon minced garlic
- Black pepper and Himalayan salt to taste
- ½ cup chopped onions

- 1/3 cup coconut flour

- 1 to 2 cups chopped celery

- 1 to 2 cups chopped carrots

- ¾ teaspoon sage

- 1 teaspoon thyme

- ¾ teaspoon rosemary

- 4 cups bone broth, chicken

- 2 to 3 tablespoons ghee

- Himalayan salt

Method:

In a bowl, mix the ground turkey, eggs, minced onion, minced garlic, onion powder, sea salt, and black pepper. Once mixed thoroughly, form into balls. In a stockpot, add onions, ghee, carrots, and celery. Cook over medium high heat until onions become translucent.

Pour the broth into the pot and simmer the mixture. Add the remaining seasonings. Drop the meatballs carefully into the broth. Cook for 45 more minutes. Serve hot.

WARMING AND CLEANSING SOUPS AND STEWS

Gut-Healing Chicken Bone Broth

You will realize how easy it is to prepare your own bone broth once you get the hang of it. You can consume this flavorful soup or use it to add an ultra-savory taste or umami to other dishes. You can add broths to sauces, stews, soups, mashed vegetables, or in stewing meats. You can also use it as a substitute for baked goods that require the use of milk or water.

Ingredients:

- 2 tablespoons lemon juice (you can also use raw apple cider vinegar)

- 3 scallions (ends trimmed)

- 2 carrots (ends trimmed)

- 4 stalks celery (ends trimmed)

- 1 tablespoon Himalayan salt

- 1 gallon filtered water

- 2 pounds pasture-raised or organic chicken drumsticks

Method:

1. Put all ingredients in a slow cooker. Set on a low and cook for 12 to 24 hours. Occasionally check and add water if needed.

2. Strain the meat and bones. You can keep the drumstick meat for another recipe.

3. Transfer broth to a container. Leave to cool, close the lid, and refrigerate. It will last up to a week in the fridge. You can consume the broth as is or add it to other recipes.

Turkey Bone Broth

This recipe is loaded with compounds known as glycosaminoglycans that aid in boosting the immune system and healing the body tissue. Turkey meat is rich in minerals and nutrients, including phosphorous, zinc, iron, potassium, and B vitamins.

Ingredients:

- 6 garlic cloves (smashed)
- 7 quarts filtered water
- 2 bay leaves
- 1 mandarin orange peel (or lemon peel)
- 1 large onion (chopped)
- 1 cup parsley
- Turkey giblets
- 1 carcass from a roasted turkey

Method:

1. Place giblets, turkey carcass, onion, bay leaves, orange peel, parsley, and garlic in a pot over medium-high flame. Add enough cold water to cover all ingredients. Bring to a boil. Reduce heat to low and leave to simmer for 10 hours.

2. Strain the solid particles. Transfer broth to jars and leave to cool. Scoop out the fat at the surface of each jar, close the lid, and freeze.

Warming Butternut Squash Soup

Yield: 6 servings

Ingredients:

- 2 tablespoons ghee (you can also use coconut oil)
- 1 large butternut squash
- Garnishing of choice
- 1 teaspoon salt (add more to taste)
- 2 cups chicken bone broth
- 1 teaspoon apple cider vinegar
- 3/4 cup coconut milk (canned)
- 1 cup water
- 1/2 teaspoon cinnamon
- 1/4 teaspoon red chili flake
- 1/4 teaspoon sumac (optional)

- 1.5-inch piece fresh ginger (chopped)

- 2 garlic cloves (chopped)

- 1/2 yellow onion (chopped)

Method:

1. Roast squash in a preheated oven at 425 degrees for 10 minutes. Flip and continue roasting for 10 more minutes. Slice in half, remove skin and seeds and slice into cubes.

2. Melt oil in a pot over medium flame. Cook onion for 5 minutes. Add ginger and garlic and cook for 1 minute. Stir in the squash and leave to cook for 10 minutes. Remove from heat.

3. Use an immersion blender to process the soup until smooth. Heat the pot over low flame. Add apple cider vinegar, coconut milk, and water. Stir and leave to cook for 2 minutes. Remove from heat and season to taste.

Put the toppings before serving.

Bone Broth with Herbs

This is a good breakfast soup since it is loaded with minerals and gelatin that help in sealing up a leaky gut. Consuming this in the morning is enough to suppress your hunger until lunch. This broth contains garlic and parsley, spices that are both antifungal and antibacterial, which fight off the bad microbes in the GI tract.

Yield: 2 servings

Ingredients:

- 1 garlic clove

- 1/2 cup zucchini (diced)

- 1 cup fresh parsley

- Salt and pepper to taste

- 2 cups ground breakfast sausage (cooked)

- 4 cups homemade bone broth

Method:

Put salt, parsley, garlic, broth, and pepper in a blender. Process until combined and smooth. Transfer mixture to a pot over medium-high flame. Stir in zucchini and leave to cook until tender. Add sausage, gently stir, and remove from heat.

Serve at once.

Super Easy Bone Broth Taco Soup

Yield: 2 servings

Ingredients:

- 1 teaspoon ground cumin
- 1 cup cilantro
- 4 radishes (thinly sliced)
- 1 avocado (diced)
- A pinch of salt
- 1/4 cup red onion (roughly chopped)
- 4 cups bone broth
- 1/2 pound cooked ground beef

Method:

1. Pour the broth in a pan over high flame. Bring to a boil. Add cilantro, cumin, and onion. Simmer for 2 minutes. Remove from heat and transfer to a blender. Process until smooth.

2. Transfer soup to serving bowls. Top with radish, avocado, and ground meat. Season with salt before serving.

Beef Osso Buco

Yield: 6 servings

Ingredients:

- 2 tablespoons sugar-free organic tomato paste (with no additives)
- 3 bay leaves
- 1 cup meat stock
- 8 beef Osso buco cuts
- 2 zucchinis (diced)
- 2 carrots (diced)
- 6 garlic cloves (crushed)
- 1/4 teaspoon oregano
- 1/4 teaspoon thyme
- 2 tablespoons olive oil
- 2 to 3 tomatoes (diced)
- 2 onions (diced)
- 1-inch piece ginger root (finely grated)
- 1-inch piece turmeric root (finely grated)

Method:

1. Put onion, garlic, tomatoes, turmeric, ginger, thyme, oregano, olive oil, and tomato paste in a food processor. Process until the

consistency is similar to a thick paste.

2. Transfer processed seasoning to a crockpot. Add meat, bay leaves, 1 cup of meat stock, and chopped vegetables. Cover and cook on a low-setting for 8 hours.

Italian Meat Casserole

You can use other meats to tweak the recipe. You can use a variety of meats, such as whole chicken, venison, quail, pheasant, joint of beef, joint of pork, shoulder of lamb, lamb shanks, or turkey legs.

Yield: 8 servings

Ingredients:

Meat and Stock

- Filtered water
- 1 lamb shoulder

For the herbs and spices

- 1 teaspoon salt
- 2 rosemary sprigs
- 4 bay leaves (or other mixed herbs of choice)

Vegetables

- 1/2 head of cauliflower (roughly chopped)
- 1/2 pumpkin (cut into cubes)

- 2 carrots (diced)

- 2 celery sticks (diced)

- 1 large onion

- 8 garlic cloves (crushed)

Method:

1. Put a little amount of duck or lamb fat in a pan over low flame. Add celery, onion, and garlic. Cook for 2 minutes while stirring often. Turn off the heat.

2. Place meat and meat joint in an oval cast iron pot. Add filtered water enough to cover most parts of the meat, keeping some parts exposed. Add the sautéed vegetables and season with salt. Add the herbs. Cover the pot and slow cook for 6 hours at 140 degrees Celsius.

3. Put the cooked vegetables to the pot. Leave to cook for 50 minutes at 180 degrees Celsius.

4. Strain the stock. You can serve it as a warm drink.

5. Put the meat and vegetables in a bowl and serve.

Creamy Healing Tomato Soup

Yield: 4 servings

Ingredients:

- 1 red bell pepper (chopped)

- 1 red onion (chopped)

- 2 tablespoons coconut oil

- Freshly ground black pepper

- 1 lime (quartered)

- 1 cup canned full-fat coconut milk

- 1 1/2 cups chicken bone broth

- 2 teaspoons curry powder

- 24 ounces canned whole tomatoes (peeled)

- 1 garlic clove (minced)

- Kosher/Himalayan salt

- 1 carrot (chopped)

- Hemp seeds and microgreens for garnish (optional)

Method:

1. Heat oil in a pot over medium flame. Add the carrot, bell pepper, and onion. Season with salt and cook for 6 minutes. Add curry powder and garlic. Cook for a minute while stirring often. Add the tomatoes. Cook for a minute and add the broth. Reduce heat to low and leave to simmer for 15 minutes. Turn off the heat. Process the soup using an immersion blender until smooth.

2. Put the pot back in the stove over medium flame. Add a squeeze of lime and coconut milk. Season with salt and pepper and cook for 1 minute.

3. Transfer to a bowl and add garnishing before serving.

Soothing Asparagus Soup

Yield: 3 servings

Ingredients:

- 1 pound fresh asparagus (trimmed and chopped)

- 3 cups chicken bone broth

- 1 tablespoon olive oil (you can also use ghee)

- 1/4 teaspoon salt

- Freshly ground black pepper to taste

- 1 small onion (roughly chopped)

- 1 small garlic clove (minced)

- 1 leek, light green and white parts (thinly sliced)

Method:

Heat oil in a pot over medium-high flame. Cook leeks, garlic, and onion until tender. Add the asparagus and season with salt and pepper. Sauté for a minute while stirring often. Add broth and simmer for 10 minutes.

Remove from heat and process using an immersion blender until smooth.

Egg Roll Soup

Yield: 5 servings

Ingredients

- 1 pound ground pastured pork
- 4 cups of broth (beef or chicken)
- 2 cups shredded carrots
- 1/2 head cabbage (chopped)
- 2/3 cup coconut aminos
- 1 onion (diced)
- 1 tablespoon olive oil
- 1 teaspoon garlic powder
- 1 teaspoon ground ginger
- 1 teaspoon Himalayan salt
- 1 teaspoon onion powder

Method:

Put meat in a pressure cooker and cook until browned. Stir in the onion and cook for 3 minutes. Add the rest of the ingredients. Lock the lid. Select the chicken/meat option and cook for 23 minutes. Release all pressure before opening the lid.

Serve at once.

Ratatouille Vegetable Stew

Yield: 6 servings

Ingredients:

- 2 green peppers (seeded and cut into strips)

- 2 tablespoons parsley (minced)

- 2 zucchinis (sliced)

- 1 eggplant (peeled and cut into cubes)

- 2 tomatoes (chopped)

- 2 garlic cloves (minced)

- 1 onion (chopped)

- 1 potato (diced)

- 4 tablespoons canola oil

- 1/4 cup chicken or vegetable stock

Method:

Put half of the oil in the pressure cooker's pot. Press any preset button and set it at 10 minutes. Add the potato, zucchini, peppers, and eggplant. Stir fry for 2 minutes and transfer to a plate. Add the remaining oil in the pot. Cook garlic and onion for 3 minutes. Put the cooked veggies back to the pot.

Lock the lid. Set the timer for 4 minutes and press the fish/vegetables steam button. Lock the lid and leave until done. Wait for all the pressure to be released before opening the lid.

Simmer for 2 minutes. Turn off the pressure cooker.

Serve immediately.

Gut-Friendly Shepherd's Pie

This pie has the right combination of ingredients that will make your gut happy. It has parsnips and carrots, root vegetables rich in minerals and prebiotics. It has spices loaded with antifungal properties, mushrooms rich in selenium, and beef that contains zinc. It also has bone broth that contains gut-sealing gelatin and bacon grease or lard with saturated fats that fight off the bad bacteria in the gut.

Yield: 4 to 6 servings

Ingredients:

- 2 tablespoons pasture-raised lard or bacon grease
- 1 pound mushrooms
- 1 pound ground organic beef
- 1 teaspoon garlic powder
- 1 teaspoon Himalayan salt
- 1 teaspoon onion powder
- 1/2 teaspoon dried ground rosemary
- 1/2 teaspoon dried ground thyme
- 1 cup bone broth

- 1 pound parsnips

- 1 pound carrots

Method:

Rinse and peel carrots and parsnips and slice into circles with half an inch thickness.

Put the bone broth in a pot over medium flame and add the sliced vegetables. Cover pot and leave to simmer for 10 minutes.

Heat lard or grease in a skillet over medium-high flame. Add mushrooms, meat, and spices. Sautee until cooked. Remove from the stove.

Transfer the cooked veggies and broth to a blender. Season with salt and process until smooth. Dollop the mixture on the cooked meat and mushroom. Stir until blended.

You can serve the dish as is. You can also place it in a preheated oven to broil if you prefer the outer crust to be crispy.

Rabbit Stew

Yield: 4 servings

Ingredients:

- 2 tablespoons extra-virgin olive oil

- 1/2 tablespoon black pepper

- 2 carrots (chunked)

- 1 rabbit (sliced into bite-size pieces)
- 1 tomato (coarsely chopped)
- 2 cups chicken broth
- 3 celery stalks (chunked)
- 12 button mushrooms (sliced)
- 2 tablespoons fresh parsley
- 1/2 teaspoon fresh rosemary
- 1 kohlrabi (chunked)
- 1 tablespoon tamari
- 2 garlic cloves (minced)
- 1 onion (chunked)

Method:

Heat oil in a pan over low flame. Add water and meat. Cook meat until both sides are browned. Add the tamari and pepper. Transfer the cooked rabbit to a baking pan. Add the tomato, kohlrabi, mushrooms, celery, and carrots.

Cook the onion in the same pan where you cooked the rabbit. Cook for a couple of minutes over low flame. Add the garlic and cook for 2 minutes. Add the broth. Scrape the bottom of the pan and mix well. Bring to a boil. Add the rosemary and parsley and cook for 2 more minutes. Remove from the stove.

Pour the mixture on top of the veggies and rabbit in the baking pan.

Bake for 45 minutes in a preheated oven at 350 degrees.

Transfer to a platter along with the pan juices. Serve while hot.

PROBIOTIC-RICH SALADS

Cauliflower Tabbouleh

Tabbouleh is a Middle Eastern staple that has a mixture of fresh flavors. Most recipes call for bulgur wheat. However, this recipe calls for cauliflower, which is one of the world's healthiest vegetables. Cauliflower is chock-full of antioxidants and anti-inflammatory nutrients. Moreover, this tabbouleh salad is low on carbohydrates.

Preparation Time: 35 Minutes

Makes 6 Servings

Ingredients:

- 1 head cauliflower (large)

- ¾ cup olive oil, extra virgin

- ½ cup lemon juice

- 1 bunch chopped green onions

- 1 bunch washed and chopped parsley

- 2 cups chopped Roma tomatoes

- 1 teaspoon pepper

- 1 teaspoon salt

Method:

Chop the cauliflower head. Place the chopped pieces into a food processor. Pulse until you get a consistency that resembles rice. Remove from the food processor. In a large bowl, combine the lemon juice and cauliflower. Stir well. Add the parsley, olive oil, tomatoes, green onions, pepper, and salt. Mix well.

If needed, add more pepper and salt. Cover the bowl and refrigerate for a minimum of 4 hours. Stir the contents once every hour.

Superfood Zucchini, Spinach, Kale & Cucumber Salad

Cucumber is not really the first choice for salad. Usually, romaine lettuce is the choice as a salad base. Why not cucumber? Cucumber has anti-inflammatory and detoxifying properties. Moreover, it has a neutral taste that will not clash with other ingredients' flavors.

Preparation Time: 40 Minutes

As a side salad, the recipe makes 5 to 6 servings. As a meal, the recipe makes three servings.

Ingredients:

- 2 teaspoons olive oil
- 1 zucchini, sliced and washed
- 6 to 8 chopped Brussels sprouts
- 1 clove garlic, minced and smashed
- 2 teaspoons cinnamon
- ¼ cup almonds
- 1 washed and sliced cucumber
- 2 cups spinach
- 2 cups kale
- 1 washed and spiralized cucumber
- 1 pitted and diced avocado

- ¼ to ½ cup raisins

- Seeds from 2 pomegranates

Dressing:

- 1 teaspoon lemon zest, grated

- 1 tablespoons lemon juice

- 1 tablespoon and 2 teaspoons honey, raw

- ¼ cup olive oil

- ½ teaspoon Himalayan salt

- ½ teaspoon pepper

Method:

Preheat the oven to 350°F. Combine the olive oil, chopped Brussels sprouts, zucchini, garlic, almonds, and cinnamon in an ovenproof dish. Bake for about 30 minutes. In a salad bowl, combine the kale, cucumbers, avocado, spinach, raisins, and pomegranate seeds. Chill while you prepare the dressing.

Mix the dressing ingredients in a medium bowl. Chill. Remove from the refrigerator the large salad bowl and mix in the dressing and the baked vegetables. Toss until the dressing has coated the vegetables. If desired, top with more raisins and pomegranate seeds.

Kale Caesar Salad

Instead of romaine lettuce, this recipe calls for the healthier kale, which provides an abundant supply of vitamins K, A, and C, and anti-inflammatory and antioxidant benefits. Pecorino Romano (from sheep's milk) and goat's milk yogurt comprise the tangy and creamy dressing's base.

Preparation Time: 25 Minutes

Makes 4 to 5 Servings

Ingredients:

- ½ cup goat's milk yogurt, full-fat
- ½ cup finely grated Pecorino Romano cheese. Set aside some cheese shavings.
- 2 teaspoons Dijon mustard
- 2 anchovy fillets or 2 teaspoons anchovy paste
- 1 teaspoon Worcestershire sauce
- Zest of 1 lemon
- 1 garlic clove, minced or pressed
- Fresh cracked pepper and salt to taste
- 10 ounces washed baby kale, patted dry afterwards
- 1 to 2 tablespoons lemon juice, to taste
- 2 sliced Roma tomatoes

- ½ cup sliced Cerignola olives
- ½ cup almonds, sliced

Method:

In a small bowl, blend or whisk together the grated cheese, yogurt, mustard, anchovies, garlic, Worcestershire sauce, lemon zest, pepper, and salt until you get a smooth consistency. Gradually add in the lemon juice. You can keep the dressing in the refrigerator for up to 3 days.

Thoroughly wash your hands. In a mixing bowl, place the baby kale and add half of the dressing. Massage the leaves until they have a darker green color.

Place on a serving dish or individual plates. Top with tomatoes, olives, Pecorino Romano shavings, black pepper (freshly cracked), and almonds.

Crab Cucumber Salad

Cucumber and celery contain electrolyte minerals and onion has rich antimicrobial properties. Crab is filled with zinc that helps in keeping the gut walls healthy. For added crunch and iodine, you can serve this salad along kelp noodles.

Yield: 2 servings

Ingredients:

- 1 tablespoon toasted sesame oil

- 2 tablespoon coconut aminos

- 2 tablespoon coconut nectar

- 2 tablespoon lemon juice

- 5 ounces fresh lump crab meat (cooked and chilled)

- 12 ounces kelp noodles (optional)

- 1/4 cup red onion (thinly sliced)

- 2 celery stalks (thinly sliced)

- 1 cucumber (thinly sliced)

Method:

1. Thinly slice all veggies and place in a bowl. Add the remaining ingredients and toss until combined.

2. Serve along with kelp noodles (or any gluten-free noodles of your choice)

Beet and Carrot Salad

Yield: 4 servings

Ingredients:

For the salad

- 3 raw grated beets

- 1/2 pound carrots (grated)

For the dressing

- 3 tablespoons olive oil

- Salt and pepper to taste

- 2 tablespoons sugar-free mustard (with no additives)

- 4 tablespoons apple cider vinegar

Method:

1. Put all the ingredients for the dressing in a bowl. Mix well. Add the beets and grated carrots. Toss until combined.

2. Refrigerate for at least 2 hours before serving.

Greek Squid Salad with Spinach

Yield: 3 servings

Ingredients:

- 1/3 cup extra virgin olive oil

- 1/2 teaspoon organic maple syrup or raw honey

- 1 1/2 tablespoons red wine vinegar

- 1/2 tablespoon freshly squeezed orange juice

- 1/2 teaspoon freshly grated orange zest

- 1/2 cup berries (chilled)

- Salt and freshly ground black pepper to taste

- 1/2 pound large squid (rinsed and sliced into thick rings)

- 1/2 pound baby spinach (trimmed)

- 1 small beet (scrubbed and trimmed)

- 1 red onion (minced)

- 1 small garlic clove (minced)

Method:

1. Put olive oil, maple syrup or honey, vinegar, mustard, orange juice and zest, and garlic in a bowl. Mix well and set aside.

2. Put water, salt, and beet in a pot over high flame. Cover the pot and bring to a boil. Reduce heat to medium and simmer for 15 minutes. Drain water and set aside.

3. Put water, salt, and squid rings in a pot over high flame. Bring to a boil. Reduce heat and cook for 5 more minutes. Drain liquid and transfer squid rings to a bowl.

4. Place the baby spinach in a plate. Arrange the beet strips, onion, and squid rings. Top with the dressing and add berries before serving.

Chicken and Pineapple Salsa-Stuffed Avocados

This recipe has avocado with anti-inflammatory properties and rich in healthy monounsaturated fats. Radish and onion are loaded with sulfur for detoxification. Pineapple contains bromelain, an enzyme needed to break down proteins. Both mango and pineapple are rich in prebiotic fibers that aid in digestion.

Yield: 4 servings

Ingredients:

- 1 tablespoon lime juice
- 1/4 cup fresh cilantro leaves (minced)
- 1 cup pineapple (diced)
- 1 cup mango (diced)
- A pinch salt
- 4 avocados (cut in half, pitted)
- 4 radishes (diced)
- 1/2 cup red onion (diced)
- 1 pound leftover chicken (shredded and cooked)

Method:

1. Put the diced radishes, pineapple, cilantro, mango, and onion in a bowl. Add a dash of salt and juice of 1 lime. Add meat and toss until combined.

2. Spoon the chicken and salsa mixture to each avocado half and serve.

Mediterranean Zucchini Pasta Salad

This pasta is filling and healthy but has low carbs so you won't feel heavy or sleepy. Bacon has monounsaturated fat and basil is rich in omega-3 fats. This recipe has ingredients loaded with prebiotic fibers, such as cauliflower, romaine, and zucchini.

Yield: 4 servings

Ingredients:

- 3 tablespoons olive oil
- 2 cups raw cauliflower (processed in a food processor into a rice-like consistency)
- 1/4 cup fresh basil (minced)
- 1/2 cup green olives
- 1 cup romaine lettuce (shredded)
- Salt and pepper to taste
- 2 avocados (diced)
- 1 pound organic bacon (with no added sugar)
- 1 large zucchini (spiralized)

Method:

1. Cook bacon in a preheated skillet over medium-high flame. Transfer to a bowl. Allow to cool before crumbling into bits. Add the remaining ingredients. Toss until combined.

Cucumber & Onion Salad

Yield: 2 servings

Ingredients:

- 2 tablespoons vinegar

- Salt and pepper to taste

- 2 cucumbers (thinly sliced)

- 1 onion (thinly sliced)

- Sour cream

Method:

1. Put the cucumber slices, onion, and salt in a bowl. Toss and leave for 5 minutes. Drain liquid and put them in paper towels to absorb excess moisture. Put in a bowl and add vinegar, sour cream, and pepper to taste. Toss salad until combined.

2. Cover the bowl and refrigerate for at least a couple of hours before serving.

Spicy Lemon & Spinach Salad

Yield: 4 servings

Ingredients:

- 4 cups fresh spinach

- 4 lemons (juiced)

- 1 teaspoon sea salt

- 2 teaspoons grated lemon zest

- A pinch of cayenne pepper

Method:

1. Put the spinach greens in a bowl. Combine the remaining ingredients in another bowl. Combine the two and toss until coated.

2. Serve at once.

Tuna, Cucumber & Avocado Salad

Yield: 6 servings

Ingredients:

- 15-ounces (3 cans) sustainably-fished tuna in oil, (drained and flaked)

- 1 cucumber (thinly sliced)

- 1 medium red onion (thinly sliced)

- 3 ripe avocado (peeled, , pitted & sliced)

- 2 tablespoons Extra Virgin Oil

- 2 tablespoons lemon juice (freshly squeezed)

- 1 teaspoon Sea/Himalayan Salt to taste

- 1/4teaspoon Black Pepper

- ¼ teaspoon Cayenne Pepper (if you like it spicy)

Method:

1. In a large salad bowl combine: drained tuna, cucumber, avocado and onion.

2. Drizzle with lemon juice and olive oil. Add salt and pepper. Toss to combine and serve.

QUICK GUT-FRIENDLY NO-BAKE DESSERTS

Strawberry and Banana Ice Cream

Yield: 4 servings

Ingredients:

- 12 organic strawberries (frozen)

- 4 very ripe bananas (frozen)

- 4 tablespoons organic coconut milk

- 2 teaspoons pure vanilla extract

- 1 tablespoon raw honey

- Toppings of choice (you can use nuts, desiccated coconut, or fresh berries)

Method:

Put all ingredients in a food processor and process until smooth.

Transfer to bowls and add toppings before serving.

Choco-Berry Pudding

This recipe contains gelatin that heals junctures of a loose cell wall in the gut. The protein powder it contains in enriching and boosts your energy. Coconut milk has antimicrobial properties and contains healthy fats.

Yield: 2 servings

Ingredients:

- 1/2 teaspoon vanilla extract
- A pinch of salt
- 2 scoops chocolate-flavored Paleo protein powder (or raw cacao)
- 4 tablespoons unflavored grass-fed gelatin
- 1 can full-fat coconut milk
- 2 dates (pitted)
- 1 cup strawberries (frozen)

Method:

Pour coconut milk in a pan over medium flame. Add gelatin and whisk until combined and the mixture is thick. Turn off the heat. Add the dates and leave to steep for 3 minutes.

Put all the ingredients in a blender and process until smooth. Transfer to small containers. Chill for at least 4 hours before serving.

Blackberry Coconut Roll-Ups

This recipe is a good snack or a meal in between meals. Apple and coconut wraps contain prebiotics while the coconut butter has caprylic acid and medium chain triglycerides that get rid of yeasts.

Yield: 2 servings

Ingredients:

- 1/3 cup fresh blackberries (sliced in half)
- 1/2 cup coconut butter
- 2 coconut flour wraps

Method:

Place 2 coconut flour wraps on a cutting board. Place coconut butter on each piece and spread all over. Add the berries and fold the wraps in half.

Choco-Almond Granola Bars

Banana flour is loaded with potassium and magnesium. Tigetnuts are actually a root vegetable that has similar taste to almonds. They are rich in protein, complex carbs, and iron. Dates add sweetness to the recipe, plus they are rich in gut-friendly prebiotic fibers.

Yield: 8 small bars

Ingredients:

- 4 scoops chocolate-flavored Paleo protein powder
- 3 tablespoons coconut oil
- 1/2 cup very ripe banana
- A pinch of salt
- 1/3 cup coconut butter
- 1/2 cup sliced Tigernuts (toasted)
- 1 cup dried chopped dates
- 1/2 cup green banana flour

Method:

Heat coconut oil and butter in a pot over medium-low flame. Add vanilla, salt, and banana. Stir until melted and combined. Remove from heat. Add the dry ingredients and mix until the mixture turns into a dough.

Transfer dough to a glass baking dish lined with parchment paper. Press the dough and spread evenly. Chill for at least 4 hours.

Slice into small bars and refrigerate until ready to serve.

Tigernut and Cassava Flour Pancakes

You can make pancakes from the recipe if you'll cook it n a pan but you can also cook it in a waffle iron to make waffles.

Yield: 5 servings

Ingredients:

- 1/2 teaspoon sea salt
- 1 teaspoon pure vanilla extract
- 2 tablespoons unflavored grass-fed gelatin
- 2/3 cup palm oil shortening (or coconut oil)
- 1 very ripe banana
- 1 1/2 cups full-fat coconut milk
- 1 teaspoon baking powder
- 1/2 teaspoon baking soda
- 1 1/2 cup cassava flour
- 1/2 cup Tigernut flour
- Water as needed

Method:

Put salt, gelatin, baking soda, baking powder, and flours in a bowl. Mix well. Set aside.

In another bowl, put banana, oil, vanilla, and coconut milk. Mix until combined.

Combine the two mixtures. Add water to make it thinner, if necessary. Leave to rest for 20 minutes.

Cook pancakes in a pan in batches. Transfer to a plate and add your preferred toppings.

Cinnamon Sugar Apples

The recipe is sweet even if it doesn't have white sugar. The natural sweetness comes from coconut butter, date, and apples, plus they are also rich in prebiotic fiber and magnesium.

Yield: 2 servings

Ingredients:

- 1 date (pitted and chopped)
- 1/8 teaspoon cinnamon
- 1/4 cup coconut butter
- 1 medium firm apple (cored and seeded)
- A pinch of salt

Method:

In a bowl, put the chopped dates, salt, cinnamon, and coconut butter. Mix well.

Slice the apple into wedges.

Serve the apple wedges with the dipping and enjoy.

Rhubarb Strawberry Popsicles

These popsicles taste good, are healthy, and are vegan-friendly. Their main ingredients are rhubarb, which is fiber-rich, and strawberries, which are loaded with antioxidants. Full-fat coconut milk makes the popsicles creamy. If you are craving for a cool treat during the summer, reach for an ice pop and enjoy.

Preparation Time: 8 to 10 Minutes

Freezing Time: 2 Hours

Makes 8 Popsicles

Ingredients:

- 1 ½ cups strawberries
- 5 to 6 rhubarb stalks
- 1/3 cup coconut milk (canned/full fat)
- ½ cup maple syrup

Method:

Chop the strawberries and the rhubarb stalks and place them in a small pot. Over medium heat, cook the fruit for around 8 minutes or until the rhubarb becomes tender. In a blender, combine the fruit mixture, coconut milk, and maple syrup. Blend on high until thoroughly combined. Fill the ice pop molds with the mixture and freeze for 2 to 3 hours. Before you serve the ice pops, run the molds for 20 seconds under warm water. This allows the pops to separate from the mold.

BONUS RECIPES

GI-Healing Juice

More people are struggling with leaky gut syndrome. Such condition can cause low energy, allergies, autoimmune conditions, weight gain, and joint pain. This recipe can help you decrease inflammation and repair the lining of your gut.

Preparation Time: 5 Minutes

Makes 2 Servings

Ingredients:

- 1 cucumber
- ½ head Napa cabbage, small
- 1 to 2 cups aloe juice
- ¼ to ½ cup mint leaves
- 1 small ginger knob (fresh), peeled

Method:

In a juicer, place the cucumber, mint leaves, and cabbage. Remove from juicer. Add in the aloe juice. Serve immediately and consume.

Gut-Healing Smoothie

Leaky gut has links to various health conditions from irritable bowel syndrome, food sensitivities, inflammatory skin conditions, and to autoimmune diseases, among other conditions. This smoothie can help heal the gut, and it is easy to prepare.

Preparation Time: 8 Minutes

Makes 4 Servings

Ingredients:

- 2 cups kale
- 1 to 2 cups almond milk or coconut milk (full-fat)
- ½ avocado
- 2 cups spinach
- 1 teaspoon ginger, freshly grated
- 2 bananas (frozen), cut into chunks
- ½ tablespoon bee pollen
- ½ tablespoon flax or chia seeds
- 1 tablespoon hemp hearts
- 2 tablespoons whey protein or collagen protein
- 1 tablespoon Manuka honey or raw honey

Method:

Put all the ingredients in a blender. Blend on high for about 2 to 3 minutes or until smooth. Pour the smoothies over ice.

Spiced Turmeric Latte

As a relative of ginger, turmeric has curcumin, which is a powerful antioxidant. Not only does curcumin provide the bright color, it also is the reason why turmeric is a healthy addition to many dishes. You can enjoy turmeric latte as a snack. You can even have it as dessert.

Preparation Time: 10 Minutes

Makes 2 Servings

Ingredients:

- ½ to 1 tablespoon turmeric
- 2 cups canned coconut milk (full-fat) or almond milk (unsweetened)
- ½ teaspoon vanilla
- 1 tablespoon ghee or coconut oil
- ½ teaspoon reishi, powdered
- ½ teaspoon ashwagandha, powdered
- ½ teaspoon cordyceps, powdered
- 1 to 1 ½ teaspoons raw honey or maple syrup
- ½ teaspoon cinnamon

Method:

In a medium pot, place turmeric, nut milk, vanilla, and ghee/coconut oil. Over medium heat, stir the mixture until it becomes hot and the ingredients well blended.

Remove from fire. Place the mixture in a blender and add cordyceps, reishi, ashwagandha, maple syrup/honey, and cinnamon. Blend on high until the mixture is smooth. Serve in mugs or cups and top with cinnamon.

Choco Chip Cookie Bars

This recipe is gluten-free and made with maple sugar instead of conventional sugar. Maple syrup is the result after sugar maple sap has boiled for longer periods than is required to make maple syrup. As most of the water has boiled off, what remains is solid sugar. Maple sugar can substitute for brown sugar.

Preparation Time: 5 Minutes

Total Time: 50 Minutes

Makes 6 Servings

Ingredients:

- 1 cup maple sugar

- 3 eggs

- 4 tablespoons melted butter

- ½ tablespoon vanilla extract

- ½ cup dark chocolate chips

- 1 can (13.5 ounces) rinsed cannellini beans, dried afterwards

- ½ cup crushed walnuts

Method:

Preheat the oven to 325°F. In a high-powered blender, add all the ingredients except the chocolate chips and walnuts. Blend on high until the ingredients have combined well. In an 8"x8" pan, pour the mixture.

Sprinkle the walnuts and chocolate chips over the batter. Bake until golden brown, around 45 minutes. Remove from oven and top with honey and coconut kefir, if desired.

Poppy Seed-Lemon Muffins

These muffins are excellent for Easter or all year round. You can have them as a dessert or served during breakfast with your eggs or gluten-free cereal. The recipe uses healthy, gut-friendly ingredients like goat milk yogurt and gluten-free flour.

Preparation Time: 35 Minutes

Makes 12 Servings

Ingredients:

- 2/3 cup coconut sugar

- ½ cup softened butter

- 2 eggs, separated

- 1 teaspoon baking powder

- 1 1/3 cups flour, gluten-free

- ½ teaspoon baking soda

- Zest of 2 lemons

- 3 to 4 tablespoons poppy seeds

- ½ cup yogurt (goat's milk-based)

- ¼ teaspoon sea salt

- 1 teaspoon vanilla extract

- 2 tablespoons lemon juice

Method:

Preheat the oven to 350°F. Cream coconut sugar and butter in a bowl. One by one, add the egg yolks, mixing well after every addition.

Mix the dry ingredients, lemon zest, and poppy seed in a separate bowl. Combine mixed dry ingredients and the butter-sugar-egg yolk mixture. Blend them slowly and continuously. Add the vanilla, lemon juice, and yogurt.

In another bowl, beat the egg whites until stiff and soft peaks form. Fold the stiff egg whites into the muffin mixture. Fill pre-lined muffin tins and bake them for 20 to 25 minutes.

Apple Galette

This gluten-free galette is similar to a tart, only that a tart is from a symmetrical pastry that has the filling added either after or before cooking. The tart also does not have a top crust. Galettes, on the other hand, are not as restrictive, and they also do not require a pie pan or pastry ring to give them shape or hold them down. You just fold them over the filling, and then bake them.

Preparation Time: 3 Hours and 20 Minutes

Makes 6 Servings

Main Ingredients:

- 2 to 3 thinly sliced apples

Flour Mixture:

- 5 tablespoons sugar (maple), divided
- 1/3 cup almonds, sprouted
- 2 tablespoons sprouted flour blend (oat, sorghum, brown rice), gluten-free

Galette Crust:

- 2 ½ cups sprouted flour blend (oat, sorghum, brown rice), gluten-free
- 1 tablespoon maple sugar
- 1 teaspoon Himalayan salt
- ¼ cup ice water

- 2 sticks unsalted butter (from grass-fed sources), cubed and chilled

Method:

In a food processor, combine the flour mixture ingredients and set aside. Add in the sprouted flour blend for the galette crust, maple sugar, and salt. While pulsing, add the butter. Mix until well combined. Gradually add the ice water. Pulse until you form a thick dough.

Roll the dough into a disc, and wrap it in cling plastic. Chill the dough for 2 hours.

Preheat the oven to 400°F. Remove the dough and roll it into a 10" to 12" circle. Coat the dough with some of the flour mix. Form the apples into a circle. Top with more of the flour mix. Fold the piecrust over the apples. Use coconut cream to brush the top of the galette. Sprinkle it with maple sugar.

Chill the galette for 25 more minutes. Bake the galette until the crust becomes golden brown or for 50 minutes to an hour.

Quinoa Krispies

With the term 'krispies,' you may assume this snack treat is made of rice, butter, marshmallows, and sugar. Fortunately, this recipe calls for the healthier, gluten-free quinoa. This snack is all about substitutions. Instead of butter as a binder, this recipe uses sunflower seed and almond butters instead.

Preparation Time: 10 Minutes

Makes 10 to 12 Servings

Ingredients:

- 3 cups quinoa or millet, puffed

- ½ cup sunflower seed butter

- 1 cup almond butter

- 3 tablespoons coconut oil

- ½ cup raw honey

- 1/8 teaspoon cinnamon

- 1 teaspoon sea salt

Method:

Line an 8"x8" baking dish with parchment paper. Set aside. Melt sunflower seed butter, almond butter, coconut oil, and honey in a small pot. Remove from heat and add in cinnamon and sea salt. Add the puffed quinoa. Mix well.

Pour the quinoa-butter mixture into the prepared dish. Use a spatula to spread out the mixture and make an even layer. For 20 minutes or longer, freeze the mixture until it is set.

When you are ready to serve, remove the krispies from the freezer. Immediately cut into desired sizes. Serve the krispies while still frozen.

Pumpkin Bread

This gluten-free snack is perfect for your afternoon tea or coffee. You can also pair the bread with a glass of non-dairy almond milk. Its texture is fluffy and it has a strong pumpkin taste and rich nutty flavor.

Ingredients:

- ¼ cup coconut flour
- 1 cup almond flour
- ½ teaspoon baking soda
- ½ teaspoon sea salt
- 1 teaspoon cinnamon
- ¾ cup pumpkin
- ½ teaspoon pumpkin pie spice
- ¼ cup maple syrup
- 3 to 4 organic eggs
- ¼ cup coconut oil, melted

Method:

Preheat the oven to 325°F. In a bowl, combine the wet ingredients. In a separate bowl, combine the dry ingredients. Mix the contents of both bowls. Mix until they are thoroughly incorporated. Pour into a loaf pan (greased) and bake for 45 to 60 minutes.

Tahini

If you are used to buying tahini at the grocery store, the notion of making your own sauce can intimidate you. Tahini is a spread/dip that is excellent with pita chips, sandwiches, or vegetables. Since it is sesame-seed based, tahini lowers blood pressure and cholesterol and protects your heart.

Preparation Time: 35 Minutes

Makes 10 Servings

Ingredients:

- ½ to ¾ cup olive oil, extra virgin
- 16 ounces sesame seeds (Bob's Red Mill is a good brand)

Method:

Preheat the oven to 350°F. Put the seeds on a baking sheet and toast them in the oven for 8 to 10 minutes. Remove from the oven and let the seeds cool for about 15 minutes.

Place the olive oil and sesame seeds in a food processor. Pulse on high, and scrape the edges for optimum mixing. Blend for 2 to 3 minutes until mixture is creamy and smooth.

Thai Chili Sauce

It is tricky finding the right sauce at the supermarket. You have to check the ingredients first to see if any of them agree with you. You need to be aware of gluten or other thickeners that may harm your gut. The recipe below takes out all the hassle of scrutinizing food labels. It is great in stir-fry dishes and on Asian-style sandwiches. You can also use it as a cracker, vegetable, and fruit dip.

Preparation Time: 5 Minutes

Makes 4 to 6 Servings

Ingredients:

- 1 cup cashew butter, raw
- 1/3 cup water
- 1 ½ tablespoon ginger (fresh), chopped and peeled
- 1/3 cup coconut sugar
- 1/3 cup lemon juice
- 1 jalapeño, with seeds and stems removed
- 4 cloves garlic, minced and crushed

Method:

Place all the ingredients in a food processor or blender. Blend on high until you achieve a sauce-like consistency. If necessary, add more water.

Tzatziki Sauce

Tzatziki is a Turkish- and Greek-based dipping sauce that usually consists of sheep or goat yogurt, and mixed with cucumber, fresh herbs, olive oil, and lemon juice. Tzatziki's etymology comes from the Turkish term 'cacik.' The term is in an Ottoman dictionary, which means an herb-and-yogurt salad. Thus, the nutritious cucumber sauce is an excellent sauce for your next Middle Eastern- or Mediterranean-inspired dish.

Preparation Time: 10 Minutes

Makes 6 to 8 Servings

Ingredients:

- 8 ounces yogurt (goat)
- ¼ cup olive oil
- ½ cucumber, chopped and peeled
- 3 cloves garlic
- 2 tablespoons fresh dill, chopped
- ½ lemon, juiced
- Paprika to taste
- ½ teaspoon sea salt

Method:

In a blender or food processor, mix the yogurt, olive oil, cucumber, fresh dill, lemon juice, sea salt, and garlic cloves. Puree or blend on high. Place the tzatziki in a serving bowl. If desired, top with paprika. Serve together with freshly cut vegetables or falafel.

FINAL THOUGHTS ON LEAKY
GUT NO MORE

W e'd like to start this finishing section by thanking you. By reading this book all the way to the end, you've demonstrated a commitment to understand your intestinal system better. This new knowledge is revolutionary in several ways. First, we can protect ourselves from diseases we were not aware the cause of in the past – one of them being the leaky gut syndrome. Secondly, it is becoming increasingly clear that food we eat can either feed the good bacteria and make us healthy, happy and full of energy, or cause chronic inflammation, obesity, diabetes, dementia, depression, cancer, cardiovascular problems and many more.

Now, before we close things out, we strongly recommend that you implement what you've learned. While it would be impossible to implement the practices and suggestions all at once, we recommend starting small. Eliminating gluten and sugar from your diet would be a good start. Slowing down and learning to properly chew your food would be another relatively easy but important step.

Healing from leaky gut syndrome is about changing your lifestyle and sticking to it. Dedicate some time and effort to learn this new lifestyle and you will be surprised by the incredible benefits of a healthy, slim and vibrant body. You already know that bloating, brain fog, belly fat and low energy levels are no fun at all. So, is it worth the effort? You know it is!

We wish you the best of luck in your journey to heal your gut forever. Now get into action!